A FAITH OF EQUAL STANDING

Adam Rebandt

Advantage
BOOKS

A FAITH OF EQUAL STANDING

A Collection of Thoughts on Justice, Race, Life and Difference

R. Adam
Rebandt III

A Faith of Equal Standing by Adam Rebandt
Copyright © 2021 by Adam Rebandt
All Rights Reserved.
ISBN: 978-1-59755-654-5

Published by: ADVANTAGE BOOKS™
                 Longwood, FL
                 www.advbookstore.com

Library of Congress Catalog Number: 2021945027

Name: Rebandt, Adam, Author
Title: A Faith of Equal Standing / Adam Rebandt
Description   Longwood: Advantage Books, 2021
Identifiers: (print): 9781597556545
            (epub): 9781597556682
Subjects: RELIGION: Christian Life - Inspirational

First Printing: September 2021
21 22 23 24 25 26   10 9 8 7 6 5 4 3 2 1

Table of Contents

Adam Rebandt

Preface

Throughout history, societies have found ways to devalue human life and ignore God's authoritative statements about our status before and obligations to Him. In Genesis 3, the serpent confused Eve's standing as an image bearer under God's authority. Ever since, people have been divided and oppressed by racial or ethnic status, age, cultural expressions and preferences, etc. This book arose out of a desire in my own life to understand and apply God's antidote to the denigration of humanity in its various forms. The Bible tells us that in Christ we have a faith of equal standing. A thorough understanding of this biblical principle provides a starting point for remedying current issues such as racial injustice, the destruction of the unborn, the poor and needy, gender confusion, and divisions over cultural differences within the church. This book is written for the Christian— the believer who follows Jesus Christ and considers himself or herself accountable to the Word of God. It should benefit anyone with an open mind but will most fully impact those who fully embrace God's Word as living and active and able to affect change. My greatest challenge in writing this book was codifying the multifaceted applications of the concept of equal standing. It seems that these observations are best presented as a collection: a grouping of self-contained chapters, each of which examines one or more aspects of how the doctrine of equal standing applies to issues within the home, the church, or the world. These chapters may be read in sequence or out of order. My hope and prayer is that they will be read and considered with personal reflection and application, and that they will ultimately lead to change in the ways we value and treat one another in diverse areas of our lives. This book's value lies in its ability to illuminate concepts from the most profitable Book of all and is therefore written with the intention of directing our attention to the timeless Word of God.

Adam Rebandt

Chapter 1

A Faith of Equal Standing – Defined and Exemplified

In 2012, my wife Sarah and I were in the process of adopting our little girls from Ethiopia. Sarah was out with a friend who was pregnant at the time. A man sitting nearby saw her pregnant friend and said, "Way to go! Way to have another white baby! It's a good thing; otherwise, the blacks will take over." All three were white, so he thought nothing of his comment. But Sarah, in the midst of adopting two African girls, was profoundly hurt by his words and their implications. When she recounted the story, I experienced a mix of emotions. At first, I was shocked, wondering how someone could actually think this way, let alone express those thoughts verbally. I could not fathom how someone could have such poor judgment. As wrong and corrupt as it would have been coming from someone who does not know Jesus, this comment came from a professing believer. After this, I began to pay close attention to the expressions, words, and reactions of others. I realized that there are latent biases in our minds and hearts that surface when we speak. In Matthew 12:34, Jesus says to the Pharisees, "*You brood of vipers! How can you speak good things, when you are evil? For out of the abundance of the heart the mouth speaks.*" Jesus was confronting the elitist mindset of the Pharisees. They believed that they had a faith of greater standing than others. They believed that they were superior because of who they were and how they behaved.

God's church cannot maintain principles against His Word and expect blessing. Jesus explains that a house divided against itself cannot stand. But Jesus will build His church, and the gates of Hell will not prevail against it. We must demonstrate that we are a part of His church, and not live contrary to the truth that He has created all men and women in His image. We can have confidence that He changes hearts. Jesus says in Matthew 12:30: "*Whoever is not with me is against me, and whoever does not gather with me scatters.*" If we have the Holy Spirit living in us, how can we participate in dividing the church and suggesting that some are better than others? When we do, we become like the Pharisees. It is absurd to think that our skin color gives us a greater standing before God. Yet many people think this way and live their lives accordingly. It is evident in the way that they associate with others and think of God's hand of blessing. More white babies? How about more black and white babies that learn to sit around the King's throne as His children? How can we hope otherwise as a follower of Christ? Obviously, people do. But how can we affect change? This book is about how God brings the hope of unity through His work in the lives of individuals.

My adopted twin girls are as much my children as my four biological sons. They have an equal standing. They are loved equally by their parents. They are loved equally by our heavenly Father and Jesus Christ, who was not only willing to associate with them, but willing to die on the cross for them. If we think we have a greater faith, a greater understanding, or a greater position because we are white, we have missed Jesus Christ and the unifying power of the Gospel. Many of us need to examine how our upbringing and assumptions have informed our beliefs.

The Word of God has been given to you and to me, and the Holy Spirit aids our discernment of his Word. The Holy Spirit does not confuse truth; Satan confuses truth. The Holy Spirit does not give one truth to Baptists and another truth to Presbyterians. The Holy Spirit does not give one truth to the black community and another to the white community, or one truth to men and another to women. We all have the same truth. That truth is God's Word. Truth is undivided: if there are two views of truth, one must be incorrect. No one has a faith of greater standing than anyone else. Our faith is not better because of the church we go to or the country we live in. I do not have a faith of greater standing because I go to Oakland Hills Community Church or because I have six children and you have five. If you have seven children, we still have an equal standing in our faith. The epistle of Second Peter was written for "*those who have obtained a faith of equal standing with ours by the righteousness of our God and Savior Jesus Christ*" (1:1). When we realize how great is the Father's love lavished on us, we are so overwhelmed by how much He loves us that we no longer focus on needing to be better than anyone else in standing. We already have the best standing, and He has given that to all of us, that we might be called the children of God.

Having obtained this faith of equal standing, Christians must identify with the words of Scripture if we are to identify with Christ. God's Word breathed out by the Holy Spirit has given one set of truth, and if we submit ourselves to God's authority, we must accept that we are all equally made in our Creator's image. Yet our world says there are many truths, and our churches are inconsistent in teaching truth. Seeing this, we might despair that the battle is overwhelming. We might give up the fight for unity by saying, "*This problem is not able to be solved, so why try?*" But perhaps it does not have to bring us to the brink of despair. It is certainly possible for humanity to be depressed or down when looking at the disunity in our churches. However, since God gives the Holy Spirit to each of us, it follows that "*in Him we have redemption through his blood, the forgiveness of our trespasses, according to the riches of his grace, which he lavished upon us, in all wisdom and insight making known to us the mystery of his will, according to his purpose, which he set forth in Christ as a plan for the fullness of time, to **unite all things in him**, things in heaven and things on earth*" (Ephesians 1: 7-10, ESV). Did you see that? Jesus unites all things, and this includes things on earth. So we can see it on this side of heaven? Absolutely! This verse leads to at least two conclusions. First of all, there is no true unity apart from Christ. Outside of Christ, things fall apart. It is only "*in Him*" that we have all of these things. Satan would like to convince us that it is possible to have unity apart from Jesus, and even unity with God apart from Jesus, because he wants us to think we no longer need our Savior. Secondly, there is complete unity shared by believers in the righteousness of our God and Savior Jesus Christ. This is the faith of equal standing. Christ came to unite all things in heaven and on earth, and he is in the process of uniting all things to Himself.

It is a basic truth of the Christian faith that we do not have a better or worse standing in Jesus Christ because of heritage, skin color, gender, physical stature, number of children, vocation, wealth, possessions, the way we interpret the Bible, music preference, age, denomination, or any other large or small detail of our lives. God loves you equally in Christ because of the gift of faith He has given you. If you disagree, it suggests that either you do not know His Word, or you do not care what His Word says. If God showed you that you were wrong in an area of your thinking or understanding of His Word, would you care to change your mind? If the God of this universe, who created you, showed you that He wanted you to think differently about something, would you be willing to do it? God did this in His Word, with the apostle Peter, and it can be an illustration for us as well.

Acts 10 shows us how God shook up and altered Peter's opinion of "the *rest of the world.*" While praying on the housetop, Peter fell into a trance and saw a sheet descending from heaven with all kinds of animals, reptiles, and birds on it. "*Rise Peter, kill and eat,*" came the voice of the Lord. "By *no means, Lord, for I have never eaten anything that is common or unclean.*" The voice came to him a second time: "*What God has made clean, do not call common*" (Acts 10:13, 14). This happened three times, and the thing was taken up at once to heaven. The day before this, an angel of the Lord had come and spoken to a Gentile soldier: "*Cornelius!*" Terrified, Cornelius said "*What is it, Lord?*" And the angel of God said to him, "*Your prayers and your alms have ascended as a memorial before God. And now send men to Joppa and bring one Simon who is called Peter. He is lodging with one Simon, a tanner, whose house is by the sea*" (Acts 10:4, 5). Cornelius did what he was asked to do. He had previously lived out justice by giving alms regularly. He was devoted to God, and consequently, his prayers had become a "*memorial*" before God. What a great example from the Word of God that our prayers do not ascend unnoticed. God hears each and every prayer of His children, and in the case of Cornelius they were a mound of remembrance before God.

At first Peter was confused about the meaning of this vision. As he contemplated it, Cornelius's men arrived at the gate and called for Peter. Peter was told by the Holy Spirit to go down and accompany them, which he did without hesitation. Keep in mind that there is always unity in the Holy Spirit. He had the ability and desire to send the same message of unity to two individuals at the same time. God was working on Peter and Cornelius with the same message. It is as though he said, "*Peter, although you are a Jew, Cornelius has an equal standing with you. Cornelius, although you are a Gentile, you have the same standing as Peter.*" As Peter accompanied the men and returned to Cornelius, Cornelius bowed down to him. Peter told him to stand up. He verbalized his equal standing with Cornelius when he said, "*I too am a man.*" Peter explained: "*You yourselves know how unlawful it is for a Jew to associate with or to visit anyone of another nation, but God has shown me that I should not call any person common or unclean. So, when I was sent for, I came without objection. I ask then why you sent for me.*" (Acts 10:28). Peter could have easily accepted physical or symbolic adoration from Cornelius, but it would have been sinful, for at least two reasons. The first was clearly stated: Peter was not God, nor to be worshiped. The second reason was that it would have presented an image of pride rather than humility. In essence he would have been saying, "*Yes, you Gentile, bow at my feet.*" God had clearly shown Peter that he should not call any person common or unclean. He came without objection and in obedience. Peter associated with the very men whom most Jews would have ostracized.

Association is a picture of equality. If Peter had seen the vision from God showing that the Jews and Gentiles were both equal in God's eyes, but had chosen not to associate with Cornelius's men or go with them, the story would have been empty and unfinished. It would have contradicted the concept of equal standing in faith through Jesus. Peter would have been saying, "*I view you as equal, but I am not willing to associate with you.*"

What about some of the differences we find in today's churches? Consider the following: "*I view you as equal. You should like my music, but I do not have to like yours. I view you as equal, but I do not want to spend any time with you.*" Some well-known churches, colleges, and even some leaders in the church into the 1980s recommended black visitors find churches with people more like them. It was fine for them to study in other universities, but not theirs. Some would say, "*The neighborhood or the school is turning color, so everything is changing*" implying that a few "*black*" people moving into a neighborhood overhauled all that was there before. In God's eyes, nothing changed. When people talk and open their mouths, myself included, it does not automatically mean that what was said is equal to truth. You may already know that, but many people lose sleep over what other people say. I have tried to practice and teach my children the art of discernment. That is, when people speak words, no matter what they are, the words should be set aside and not given instant credibility. We should sift all words through God's Word and ask, "*Does God's Word support this ideology or principle?*" If so, then we can welcome it into our minds and hearts, grow with it, and be encouraged by it. It is a godly exhortation. If it does not line up with God's Word, however, then it should be cast aside as worthless, a blowing of the east wind. Unfortunately, much talk is worthless. Just because something is said does not mean that it is true or that it should ever have been verbalized. God calls us all to have a discerning mind.

In Acts 10, Peter and Cornelius, and those with them, showed discerning minds subservient to God. They set aside roadblocks of separation that had existed in their minds as to how they should view one another. They set aside their biases for God's best. They recognized God's awesome plan, His gift of the Holy Spirit to all who receive Jesus by faith, and they accepted each other as equals. In Acts 10:45, we read, "*and the believers from among the circumcised who had come with Peter were amazed, because the gift of the Holy Spirit was poured out even on the Gentiles.*" These Jews who came with Peter were now able to see the Holy Spirit poured out on the Gentiles.

Peter saw God's goodness and purpose for all believers, but his work was just beginning. Acts 11 provides an account of Peter's return to Jerusalem, the religious center of the Jews. Verses 2-3 read: "*So when Peter went up to Jerusalem, the circumcision party criticized him, saying, 'You went to uncircumcised men and ate with them.'*" The Jews were decrying Peter's association with Gentiles. Peter had not done this accidentally. He sought them out and ate with them. Remember, the Spirit told Peter to go to the Gentiles without hesitation. The circumcision party in Jerusalem, which had been dwelling on it for some time in their own minds, believed that he should have deliberated on it.

Out of the abundance of the heart the mouth speaks. These Jews criticized Peter for eating with Gentiles. They thought, "*We are better than them, but you associated with them. We are not sure we should associate with you if you keep on doing this.*" Peter and the Jews who had traveled with him, as well as the circumcision party in Jerusalem, were all Christians. However, they had different views of acceptable association. Did the Holy Spirit permit this sort of division? Of course not. The Holy Spirit that lived in Peter is the same Holy Spirit that lived in those circumcised criticizers of Peter. The same Holy Spirit lives in me and lives in you if by faith you have accepted Jesus.

Peter explained to the Jews in Jerusalem what he had experienced that made this association acceptable. He started with the vision and his interaction with the Spirit. Remember how the Spirit commanded Peter to go with the Gentiles without hesitation? In Acts 11:12, the scriptures use a different word in Peter's explanation of the events in Acts 11:12. "*And the Spirit told me to go with them, making no distinction.*" No distinction. Did you catch that? No hesitation, no distinction, no difference. Equal. Perhaps at this point the Jews of the circumcision group began contemplating these events and the possibility of changed minds.

Unity underlies this passage. Peter has their attention, and he continues in Acts 11:15-16: "*As I began to speak, the Holy Spirit fell on them **just as on us** at the beginning. And I remembered the word of the Lord, how he said, 'John baptized with water, but you will be baptized with the **Holy Spirit**.'*" Peter witnessed the outpouring of the Holy Spirit. The Holy Spirit was being poured out on all believers. In each church that professes Jesus Christ as Savior, unity should be the rule rather than the exception, for the Holy Spirit is poured out on us all.

In the next verse Peter says, "*If then God gave the same gift to them as he gave to us when we believed in the Lord Jesus Christ, who was I that I could stand in God's way?*" He was explaining to his circumcision counterparts that God is the authority. How could he stand in the way of God's Word? It was also a challenge to them: "*How can **you** stand in God's Way?*" Well, they couldn't stand in God's way. They were speechless, with no further objection or response. Acts 12:18 says, *"When they heard these things, they fell silent"*. And they glorified God, saying, *"Then to the Gentiles also God has granted repentance that leads to life."* It was as if they laid down their division, and in unison, raised their right hands together in full support of that which they had just opposed a few moments earlier. Only the Holy Spirit can bring that about! In 2 Peter 1:1, Peter writes about his *"faith of equal standing with ours"* experience from Acts 10-11, explaining how God provides a faith of equal standing, through Jesus Christ's righteousness, to all who believe. If Peter and the first century church were able to find unity in faith, can the Holy Spirit do the same with today's church? The answer is, of course.

Chapter 2

Three-Fifths –
The Enemy of Equal Standing

God is the boss, and Jesus is fully God. That is established. Yet since the beginning of time, Satan's goal has been to have the human race and God's people question God's authority. Satan wants us to devalue Jesus similarly to how he has, throughout history, made us devalue one another. Unlike some of his more subtle workings, Satan has not bothered to mask these views, but has openly attacked humanity. Nevertheless, in our fallen state, we need the Holy Spirit to open our eyes to see it. Let's take a look together.

Paul tells us that we are not unacquainted with the devil's schemes. The events of history clearly illustrate these depraved schemes to the believer who studies them with prayer and through the light of God's Word. What I will share with you will solidify a picture of what Satan is trying to do, and it will make it a little easier to answer questions of how or why horrible things occur in the world of men. Travel with me on a trip that my family recently took to Washington D.C. During our homeschool history tour vacation, we visited amazing places… The White House, the Pentagon, Capitol Hill (going into the Senate Chamber while they were in session), the Supreme Court (seeing all nine justices in the court room in session), coffee hour with one of our Senators, the Washington Monument, Arlington Cemetery, Mount Vernon and George Washington's home, the Vietnam Memorial, the Lincoln Memorial, and the Jefferson Memorial, among others. In any one of those places we experienced solemn attitude, thankful gratitude, education, and in some cases just enjoyment. However, as impactful as all of those sites were, there were four more that had an even more profound impact on me. Three of them (the African American Museum, the Native American Museum, and the Holocaust Museum) conveyed the devil's consistent method through history for destroying humanity, and one (the Museum of the Bible) pointed to the Book that tells us all that we need to know.

The first three of those museums were full of history about the struggles of one group of people against another. The African American Museum detailed the history of slavery and its ideologies in our early heritage. It was interesting to learn about the historical components of Three-Fifths Compromise as well as the symbolic meaning it has taken on since. During the 1787 Constitutional Convention, the northern states proposed this compromise as a way to limit the power of the southern states by reducing their congressional representation. Even though the enslaved population was not allowed to vote, the southern states wanted their full population to count towards their representation in Congress so they could pass laws that would benefit the southern slave owners. By counting the enslaved population as three-fifths of its actual number, the northern states limited the number of southern congressmen and therefore their power to perpetuate and expand slavery. Despite its origin as a way to limit slavery, the notion of "three-fifths" has taken its place in the collective American consciousness as a powerful symbol of the systemic devaluing of African Americans. Even after the slaves were freed at the end of the Civil War, dark-skinned people were treated as less than human. The "separate but equal" doctrine argued that people could have equal standing under the 14th amendment of the Constitution even while segregated. This legal standard gave lip-service to the idea of racial equality even among racial groups that were separated in areas of life ranging from education to drinking fountains. But the very act of separating predetermined spaces pointed to a lack of equality. It wasn't until 1954 that the Supreme Court stated, in a ruling reminiscent of God's lesson to Peter in Acts 10-11, that separation is "inherently unequal" (Brown v. Board of Education of Topeka, 1954). A true equality is without distinction and without hesitation. An unwillingness to associate is opposed to an equal view of one another. The enemy begins his work by causing us to view ourselves as higher than each other.

Tuck this away in your mind for a moment as we move on to the Native American museum. When the pioneers began settling North America and moving westward, the Native Americans were already living in many of the places that our young country desired to occupy. Three quotes from two prominent American figures reveal the sentiment that governed us during these days. Thomas Jefferson, our third president, said in a letter to George Rogers Clark on January 1st, 1780: *"The end proposed should be their extermination, or their removal"* when speaking of the tribes and Native Americans. (The Native American Smithsonian Museum exhibit). Our 7th President, Andrew Jackson, made numerous statements revealing his heart towards Native American people. In 1830 he said, *"and is it supposed that the wandering savage has a stronger attachment to his home than the settled, civilized Christian?"* On May 28th of this same year, President Andrew Jackson signed into law the Indian Removal Act. On December 3rd, 1833, Jackson also said that *"they have neither the intelligence, the industry, the moral habits, nor the desire of improvement which are essential to any favorable change in their condition. Established in the midst of another and a superior race, and without appreciating the causes of their inferiority or seeking to control them, they must necessarily yield to the force of circumstances and ere long disappear."* Jackson believed he represented members of a predominant and inherently superior race to the Native American and concluded that the Native Americans must disappear. He judged that they did not have the qualities or attributes to make them fully human, and therefore they should be removed. This way of thinking illustrates that next step in the enemy's tactics: actionable removal of the *"lesser"* out of society. But didn't God create us all equal in His image?

The enemy's end goal is destruction. He labels people inferior, enslaves or removes them, and ultimately destroys them. Satan's handprints were all over the injustice on display at the United States Holocaust Museum. As in the other two museums, our first impression was the profound injustice of the hand of the mighty against the weak. We began our time at this museum at an exhibit called *"Remember the Children: Daniel's Story"* (ushmm.org). The short tour guided us through the diary and thoughts of a young person during the Nazi persecution of the Jews: the stops along the way, the scarcity of food, and the dehumanization, all from the perspective of a child. Our only hope in the face of this evil is our God who moves on behalf of the oppressed. The Jews needed a deliverer, as do we. The sentiment of hatred for the Jews advanced by Hitler was propounded by lies. These lies were rooted in fear and meant to instill fear in the Germans that if they did not exterminate the Jews, they themselves would be destroyed. Hitler's words are profoundly disturbing. This book is intended to share the truth of God's Word, and I pray that the worst of the kingdom of darkness, through stark contrast, helps us see the Kingdom of Light. Let's look at three stages of Hitler's movement from evil towards greater evil.

The first stage is presented as a "*question*" — a rhetorical device intended to verbally welcome Hitler's listeners into his depraved ideology. The birth of the lie mirrors the original words of Satan— "*Did God really say?*" As you read the following portion of the museum's content, you can see this question behind the rhetoric: "*Did God really say that the Jews should be allowed to reproduce and trod the earth seeing as they are not as special as you are, you favored ones of Aryan descent?*" Hitler called his comment the "*Jewish Question*": "*On September 16th, 1919, Hitler issues his first written comment on the so-called Jewish Question. In the statement, he defined the Jews as a race and not a religious community, characterized the effect of a Jewish presence as a 'race-tuberculosis of the peoples,' and identified the initial goal of a German government to be discriminatory legislation against Jews. The 'ultimate goal must definitely be the removal of the Jews altogether'*" (ushmm.org. "*Adolf Hitler Issues Comment on the 'Jewish Question'*").

In the second stage, Hitler's "*question*" becomes a problem that needs a solution. Nearly a year later, in August 1920, the seed inside of Hitler has begun to grow:

> *That our people be set free, that these chains be burst asunder, that Germany be once again the captain of her soul and master of her destinies, together with all those who want to join Germany. (applause) And the fulfillment of this first demand will then open*

up the way for all the other reforms. And here is one thing that perhaps distinguishes us from you [Austrians] as far as our programme is concerned, although it is very much in the spirit of our things: our attitude to the Jewish problem.

When Satan questioned Adam and Eve in the Garden of Eden about whether or not God really said something, he created a false premise presented as a problem: "you *won't be like God*!" The answer is at hand: "*I'd better eat from that fruit to solve the problem.*" But a problem never existed in the first place that needed to be solved. Hitler continued,

For us, it is a problem of whether our nation can ever recover its health, whether the Jewish spirit can ever really be eradicated. Don't be misled into thinking you can fight a disease without killing the carrier, without destroying the bacillus. Don't think you can fight racial tuberculosis without taking care to rid the nation of the carrier of that racial tuberculosis. This Jewish contamination will not subside, this poisoning of the nation will not end, until the carrier himself, the Jew, has been banished from our midst. (applause) (D Irving, The War Path: Hitler's Germany 1933-1939. Papermac, 1978, p.xxi). (phdn.org "Concerning Jews and Judaism").

The third and final stage shows the consistency of the devil's schemes. Listen to the finality of Hitler's comments. He has gone from a question to a problem, then finally to absolute extermination. In a conversation with Josef Hell in 1922, Hitler responded to the question of what he would do if he had freedom and power to act against the Jews:

If I am ever really in power, the destruction of the Jews will be my first and most important job. As soon as I have power, I shall have gallows after gallows erected, for example, in Munich on the Marienplatz-as many of them as traffic allows. Then the Jews will be hanged one after another, and they will stay hanging until they stink. They will stay hanging as long as hygienically possible. As soon as they are untied, then the next group will follow and that will continue until the last Jew in Munich is exterminated. Exactly the same procedure will be followed in other cities until Germany is cleansed of the last Jew!" (Source: John Toland, Adolf Hitler. London: Book Club Associates, 1977, p. 116).

The end goal is evident: death. Satan lied to Adam and Eve when he told them that they would live forever if they ate. They were already designed to live forever, but Satan created a lie that brought about death. His goal has always been to separate people from God. Satan essentially created a picture of his vision of destruction in the life of Adolf Hitler. Hitler wanted physical destruction in his conversation with Hell; Satan aims for eternal separation from God, Hell itself, the worst death of all.

Satan begins with seeds of doubt that question the value of a person. He had Adam and Eve question their value, using comparison as a tool. He essentially said, "*Adam and Eve, you are only three-fifths of a person compared to God, and you need to be like God; you must eat.*" The lie led to their sin and ultimately to the curse of death. I wonder if in a short number of years, we will have the Museum to the Unborn. Satan has created the questions: "*Do you really need this baby?*" "*Can you take care of this baby?*" "*Is this baby really a person?*" "*Won't you be happier without this baby?*" "*Isn't your career more important than having this baby?*" "*It is your body, isn't it?*" "*Can't you make your own choice?*" Hitler would have called these "*The Baby Questions.*" Satan already has. The evil tactician has been mightily at work in our country. The questions have led to a nation with a problem that needs solving. "*This tuberculosis of flesh will impede the rest of MY life. What must I do now as I have this problem to contend with?*" The answer is destruction: "*I must kill it. I must hang it on one gallows after another. I must kill each one until the problem is exterminated. I must follow exactly the same procedure in every city until the U.S. is cleansed of the last unwanted baby*". When will every citizen of God's kingdom understand that the conversation and ideologies coming from culture against God are a path to hell? The question may seem innocent. The problem may seem justifiable. But in the end Satan stops at nothing short of hell.

Chapter 3

The Heavens –
God's Natural Authority Displayed

Satan doesn't want us to look around at the obvious beauty and authority displayed by God. The heavens are God's heavens, declaring His glory. Satan sets himself against God's heavens, for they declare the Creator's might and glory, which opposes his depravity and equalizes humanity under God's authority. But God's voice has spoken in His Word and through creation, and we should invest our lives in hearing God's voice clearly. Our voices are untrustworthy, but God's Word speaks clearly, and God's power is revealed through His creation, as long as we take the time to see it.

There are two kingdoms at work in the world, but they are not equal. Jesus and His Word will always reign supreme. Satan, although desirous of being God and wanting to thwart God's plans, will always be inferior to God. Satan's ideologies, therefore, will always be inferior and inadequate compared to God's ideologies. Satan is finite, God is infinite. We see examples everywhere of God's matchless power. If you pay attention to your surroundings, you will see situations in your own life in which God exhibits His power. Something as simple as daily weather, which is beyond our control, displays this power. Join me on a hike where smoke and hail and rain reminded me of God's might. In 2017, my family drove to Yosemite Valley. Smoke from nearby forest fires filled the entire valley, blocking our visibility, but thankfully cleared in time for us to hike up the Mist Trail at Yosemite. About a half mile up, I received a weather advisory with large warnings and exclamation points and thought, *"Are they really trying to tell me that there will be a storm here? How do they know where I am? It must be meant for someone else.*" I ignored the warning, and we continued the uphill hike for another 30 minutes, when suddenly, over the mountains, it began to hail. It hailed hard, large, painful pellets. We had no way to protect our heads, and it just kept coming. I remember thinking, "*I really need to be somewhere other than here right now,*" but the only shelter was back the way we came. As we descended, the temperature began to warm, and the hail turned into a downpour. My wife Sarah, my four sons Caleb, Justin, Levi, and Luke (thankfully my two young daughters were in Michigan with my parents), my mother-in-law Linda and brother-in-law Matthew all cautiously retreated. We traversed the trail carefully as streams of water covered the path. When we reached the car, it took 30 minutes for us all to change. Our new hiking boots became unusable trophies until we found a dryer. When it rains, we must take cover and find shelter. There is nothing that we can do to stop the work of God, and there is nothing Satan can do to stop the power of God. Satan only has what power God allots him, as we see in the book of Job. We cannot send smoke or clear smoke. We cannot send rain or clear rain. The smoke and rain belong to Him. God reigns over creation in every way.

When we recognize how far God our Creator stands above us, our differences become null; we are all just creatures under His glorious authority. The Bible tells us that God is in heaven and will remain there forever. He does not seek reelection. He is the King forever, hallelujah, and the heavens are His. Psalm 73:25 says, "*Whom have I in heaven but you? And there is nothing on earth that I desire besides you.*" Asaph, the author of this psalm, had a heart that sought to bring heaven to earth, similar to our supplication in the Lord's Prayer that God's will be done on earth as it is in heaven. We have the inspired Word of God to tell us how God, the Creator, intends His world to operate. His expectations, however, are rarely upheld by his creation. Christians, different from the world, desire to live in a place where God's expectations become reality, and we pray for a world that looks more like heaven, where sin diminishes, and where there is absolute equality and justice.

The desire for justice comes from being made in the image of God. It prods our heart to say, "*I know it shouldn't be like this!*" This desire is a part of the Christian's heart because the Holy Spirit lives in us, and this desire will always be there for those whose eyes are set on Christ. It is acceptable to feel a righteous indignation, especially as a member of the church. It is acceptable to think, *"That's not right,"* because this indignation comes from the Father's image on our hearts.

God also feels indignation. Psalm 7:11 says *"God is a righteous judge, and a God who feels indignation every day."* The word *"indignation"* in the Bible is used of God's hatred for sin as well as His desire to help the afflicted. The previous verse lends context, saying that God is a shield who saves the upright in heart and a God who establishes the righteous. God opposes the proud but gives grace to the humble. Examples throughout the first few chapters of Isaiah portray a God that does not hide who He is or what He is all about. In Isaiah 1:17-18, God implores Judah to seek justice and to correct oppression. How can you spread your hands to heaven and expect God to hear any of your prayers? Bring justice.

For true and godly justice to take root in our world, it must first take root in the hearts of believers. God must be King in our lives, so that His authority takes root in us and we delight to be His servants and to treat others with equality. We must care so much that we make it a priority each day. We do not have too much to do today. This is His world, and we should be on His schedule, caring about what He cares about. We should be of the mindset that we can trust Him with what we get done and do not get done. God is a refuge, an ever-present help in time of need. He is the help. So go and sit at the King's feet.

We all have things we want to see God do. We want to see Him answer prayer, but do we really pray? Psalm 144:3-5 is an inspiring petition to God. The verses begin by explaining how small we are and then shift all the focus where it belongs, on God. *"Bow Your heavens O Lord and come down! Touch the mountains so that they smoke!"* God, do something! Change our land! This prayer of David preserves the cry of David's heart. His desire was to see God do what mattered most to God. When is the last time that you prayed like that? Is a scattered minute in your waking hour for breakfast really showing your true devotion to your God and King, acknowledging Him as Lord and Sovereign over your life, or is it a matter of duty because you know you should spend more time with Him, but you've got to get started on your day? Do you tell yourself that you have too much to do? God will certainly understand how busy you are, right? God does understand how busy we are. The Scriptures are full of references to people like Elijah who was a common man just like us. However, he earnestly prayed that it would not rain, and it did not. God responds to and rewards those who earnestly seek Him. He answers the prayers of those who cry out to Him day and night. The parable of the persistent widow shows that by constant asking even an unrighteous judge will render a favorable ruling to an oppressed woman even when he does not want to, just so he will not be bothered anymore. How much more will God hear and answer His children who cry out to Him day and night?

We have longings and desires for things we want to see accomplished, big things. We see injustices that plague our life, our land, the world, and we want to see God move in these things. As we read through Scripture, we see that God stirs individuals to do great things for Him. Maybe he is calling you to be a vessel for His great work. Unless you see the wisdom in going to God first, you have missed the point of your existence. How gracious is our God that He takes the time to teach us this, and even makes Himself attractive to us through His kindness and His creation? When you pray from the heart like David did, you are coming from a point of complete humility, asking God to do what He wants, and trusting in faith that He will answer with what is best for you. And He will!

God's power, not ours, is at work in the world everywhere. *"O LORD, what is man that You regard him, or the son of man that you think of him? Man is like a breath; His days are like a passing shadow"* (Psalm 144:3-4, ESV). In this psalm, David reflects on how small he is before God. If there is one thing that all flesh should be able to regard and to relate to, it is how small we are. Think of lying on your back and looking at the stars, or standing before the vastness and breadth and depth of the Grand Canyon. A friend of mine once described his visit to Half Dome before he became a Christian. Half Dome is a famous hiking destination in Yosemite National Park that at its highest point leads to a cliff 5,000 feet above the Yosemite Valley. My friend crawled out to the edge and his buddy held his legs because he was afraid that he was going to be sucked in. Taking in the immensity of it all, he realized at that moment that this could not have formed randomly. Since then, God has fully revealed himself to this man and has allowed him to be an encouragement to many, including myself. When we open our eyes, look, and pay attention, we will see countless examples of God's power displayed right in front of us. These particles of His might will be more than we can handle! The inequality between God and us makes us wonder what God could even want with us, but it also emphasizes the reality of our equal standing under His authority and might.

God has told us exactly who He is in His Word, who we are in relation to Him, and what He expects of us. He is the Alpha and the Omega. Everything starts and ends with Him. He is omniscient. God says in Psalm 50, "*I know all the birds of the hills, and all that moves in the field is mine.*" (Psalm 50:11). He knows all things. In Genesis 1:21-25, we read that after creating the beasts of the field and birds of the air, God saw that it was good. He then created humans in His image, male and female He created them. He knows all of the beasts of field, all the birds of the air. Jesus calls us to "*look at the birds of the air: they neither sow nor reap nor gather into barns, and yet your heavenly Father feeds them. Are you not of more value than they?*" (Matthew 6:26). But it is the image of God in us that separates us from the beasts of the field and birds of the air. We have a soul and the ability to discern good from evil. We have a conscience. God has set eternity in the hearts of men. The Holy Spirit tells us through God's Word that He is in charge, and that it is God who made the heavens and the earth. We struggle daily to keep our emotions and feelings in line with God's desires. This is our flesh. Our flesh often tells us to do something differently than what the Holy Spirit has revealed in the Word of God that we ought to do. At the end of the day, look back, and you will see, as I do, that in each 24-hour period our flesh battles with the spirit. I take this as another proof that He is God and that we are not. In other words, we are not consistent in our being and how we want to act. We continue to sin and show a lack of control over ourselves. God, in contrast, always has perfection in His being. He never struggles in His attributes; He is His attributes. He is also the Creator: in the beginning, God created the heavens and the earth. He created them, and they belong to Him. He is perfect, and leads each of His creation with a perfect plan.

One of the verses that began changing my outlook on God's leading is Judges 13:25: "*And the Spirit of the Lord began to stir [Samson] in Mahaneh-dan, between Zorah and Eshtaol.*" It may seem like a simple verse about God leading Samson, but did you notice that the Spirit of the Lord began to stir him? We hear people say that you need to find your inner strength. Where does this inner strength originate? It originates with God, from the Spirit of God who lives within us. God changes hearts and desires through the Holy Spirit whom He gives to us through faith in Jesus Christ. He gave us His Holy Spirit; He put His Holy Spirit in us. The world cannot comprehend the truth of the Gospel or what it means to have the Holy Spirit living in us, but perhaps God may use this as a tool to point them to the Word of God that they too may understand what this faith of equal standing is all about. "*God, please stir me in my inner man or woman to care about what you care about.*" We must recognize that God is the Supreme Being, that the heavens are His, and that He wants to use us to bring justice and peace to His world.

Chapter 4

Hostility

The struggle is real inside each one of us. We need Him stirring us, or we are left unstirred for His good purposes. We recall what God did in the early church in the book of Acts, and we must apply godly equality in the modern era of the church. Otherwise, we continue to entropy into human nature's inclination towards inequality. Clearly the problem of inequality remains unsolved. Perhaps the solution was given to us in the book of Acts: "*God gave the same gift to them as he gave to us when we believed in the Lord Jesus Christ.*" At the risk of minimizing the greatest gift of God given to us equally at the cross, imagine two children at Christmas being given the same gift, then fighting over them. Are we to judge the suitability of the other person to receive the same gift? Is it not in the hands of the giver to determine who is suitable? Am I really willing to hit you, beat you over the head, and call you names for something WE have already been given equally? Can you say to someone, "*You are not suitable to receive the same gift that I have received, because you are 3/5 of me. And this worth is determined on my scale, for my purposes.*"? Anyone with such a view does not realize the equally small size they and we all are, or the absurdity of proclaiming our own version of God's perfect value judgment. We are all equally unqualified to redefine God's standards. It is time for us equally small creatures to join the eternal and perfect realm of God's Word.

Hostility is still a problem in our world, and even in our churches. We must first resolve the problem in the church before we can apply the gospel to the problems of the world. Ephesians 2:15-16 ESV speaks of Christ: "*by abolishing the law of commandments expressed in ordinances . . . He might create in himself one new man in place of the two, so making peace, and might reconcile*

us both to God in one body through the cross, thereby killing the hostility."
Hostility in this context is not just referring to violence but refers to more
subtle hostilities than walking up and punching someone in the face out of
anger. Just as someone needs forgiveness for this kind of blatant hostility, we
need forgiveness for the gentler ones that we so carefully hide from one
another. We may be gentle in the ways we are hostile, but gentle hostilities
that simmer because of our sinful thoughts or actions, and leave God out,
often lead to consequences in our relationship with Him and with each other.
He who tests the motives and intentions of the heart has the ability to bless our
relationships when our heart motives are in line with His.

Both the church and the world have to deal with wrong actions; we just
call those actions by different names. Immorality defined by God's word is
adultery, and as defined by the world is "criminal sexual conduct." Those
outside the church want to solve actions on the level of "crime." Christians see
immorality on a deeper level as sin against our neighbor and against God.
Non-believers can only address the action as a "crime", and therefore have no
idea how to change the heart problem that leads to certain behaviors. Non-
believers look for answers to solve "crime," not knowing what to do with sin.
They have no understanding that sin can only go away at the cross. Hearts can
only be changed by Jesus. In a 1952 article entitled "Society and The
Criminal," M. J. Sethna argued that by eliminating greed, avarice, and envy
from the human mind, we could eradicate crime from society. I applaud
Sentha for recognizing the problem apart from Christ and pointing toward
the solution. But when I first read this, I immediately thought: "*Dr. Sentha, it
is not possible to eliminate these sinful desires from the human mind.*" Romans
1:28-32 says,

> *And since they did not see fit to acknowledge God, God gave them up
> to a debased mind to do what ought not to be done. They were filled
> with all manner of unrighteousness, evil, covetousness, malice. They
> are full of envy, murder, strife, deceit, maliciousness. They are
> gossips, slanderers, haters of God, insolent, haughty, boastful,
> inventors of evil, disobedient to parents, foolish, faithless, heartless,*

ruthless. Though they know God's righteous decree that those who practice such things deserve to die, they not only do them but give approval to those who practice them (ESV).

Furthermore, Romans 8:7 says "*the mind that is set on the flesh is hostile to God, for it does not submit to God's law; indeed, it cannot*" (ESV). This mind set on the flesh is hostile to God, and eventually God gives these people up to a debased mind. Romans is speaking of those who neither glorify God as God or give thanks to Him. We are fallen creatures full of sin, and surely not able to remove this from the minds of men. Dr. Sentha recognized the solution, eradicating these things from the mind. But recognition of what the solution was, without understanding the only path to get there, will leave man in a helpless estate until the Savior appears in the person.

Do you see the problem we have here? The world offers empty solutions to spiritual problems: self-help books, training, community service, money, friends, less alcohol, fewer drugs, less sugar, less caffeine, stricter rules, etc. But Romans 12:2 says, "*Do not be conformed to this world, but be transformed by the renewal of your mind, that by testing you may discern what is the will of God, what is good and acceptable and perfect.*" Our mind is renewed when it lacks spot or wrinkle or any other type of imperfection and is holy and without blemish. It is only accomplished through faith in Jesus Christ and the washing of water with the Word of God. It is not possible all of the time here on this earth because of our sinful nature but discerning the right decision from a renewed mind shows the power of God is real!

The hostility of indifference is another way to measure where your heart is. Ephesians 5:11 says, "*Take no part in the unfruitful works of darkness, but instead expose them*" (ESV). These unfruitful works of darkness become visible when exposed by light. It is not enough to quietly disapprove of unfruitful works of darkness when our King Jesus calls us to expose them. Perhaps we need to speak more truth. If I was the pastor of a church, and I did not speak out against abortion, I would be failing to preach the whole counsel of God. How is it possible that our leaders have let this sin of failing to preach against abortion creep into the church? Maybe the enemy has deceived us as he did in the garden when he asked, "*Did God really say not to do that?*" We must remember that it is God's church. He raises up and deposes leaders. He grows His church with the bold preaching of His Word. I pray that He only raises up godly pastors who care for the unborn and speak out against abortion and that he deposes those out of the pulpit who refuse to speak this truth, unless they change by attending to His Word.

It is important that those considering abortion know that we would adopt their child. When we condone actions such as abortion in our churches, either by approval or indifference, we are essentially saying, "*I am not here to help you. I have too much going on. I hate you. I do not love you enough to speak truth to you. I want you to bear the weight of this for the rest of your life. I want you to be a fugitive until death, suffering from the pain of the consequence of this sin of destroying your child.*" Praise God he sent Jesus who forgives even those burdened with such a painful loss. But to the church leader or pastor, can you imagine a young woman coming back later and saying in anger, anguish, and helplessness, "*You knew all this would happen, and the emotions that I would go through, and my child is not here today! He or she would be 16 today! You knew this and you did not warn me.*" Although still responsible for her own actions, she was not given wise counsel from God's Word.

Is this not the same reaction that our co-workers will have one day while being tormented in Hell while we enjoy the loving peace and rest of our heavenly Father and the fellowship with the Lamb, the Lord Jesus Christ? "*You knew all of this, and you were hostile to me and showed great hate by knowing, and yet not proclaiming the Gospel.*" I know this sounds extreme, but it is serious. We need to think less about how our message will be received now, and more about how its absence affects their eternity later. Let us become experts in proclaiming the truth, the Gospel, not compelled by duty but by passion. This passion for speaking truth will only come from a close walk with our Lord, so close that we are unwilling to hide His truth. "*You had to let me die to find out that God and His Word were in the right, and you never told me?*" Our job is to share the gospel. The knowledge that we are all equally unable to determine how God might work helps us to share the gospel equitably and unrestrainedly.

When we speak truth, hostility ceases, for the gospel is the path of peace. Hostility was nailed to the cross when Jesus died for truth and when He was raised to life. Our faith in Him takes resentment away. He died to save us because Hell is real. He died to save us and offer forgiveness and healing for the woman who has had abortion. He died to offer His truth to the woman thinking about getting an abortion so that she might not go through with it because in Jesus she sees truth and hope. She knows that He will never leave her or forsake her.

I recently had a conversation with a dear companion in the faith about the failure of pastors and church leaders to speak out against abortion. These leaders refuse to acknowledge that a child in the womb is of equal value to themselves and to the mother who carries that unborn child. While understandable that those outside of Christ may come to different conclusions, it is incomprehensible that those who claim to be believers, let alone ordained pastors and leaders, can hold such a position. These conclusions lack truth and wisdom. Perhaps these churches may not want to have a young woman in the church who cannot "afford" to raise a child. What about women who want to pursue a career instead of giving birth and raising a child? A woman faced with an unexpected pregnancy may believe that if she has the baby she carries, and does not abort it, then she will have a hard, financially burdened road ahead of her. Is this a reason to give up her child forever? This is Satan's lie, as all children are a gift and God is the provider. This mindset comes from Satan and sin rather than from God. John 6:63 says, "*It is the Spirit who gives life, the flesh is no help at all.*" I love that verse. God alone brings about life; you and I are no help at all. If we adopt the mindset that children do not matter to God, we make ourselves God. We believe we must have had something to do with it, and we make the decision for that child because we believe, without knowing, that he or she will have a difficult life. God has a problem with that, and so should we.

Conception is granted by the Spirit who gives life. God plans life. A man and a woman may be trying or not trying to have a child, but in either case it is the Creator of everything who grants the beginning of a life. Psalm 139:13-16 articulates this clearly:

For you formed my inward parts; you knitted me together in my mother's womb.

I praise you, for I am fearfully and wonderfully made. Wonderful are your works; my soul knows it very well.

My frame was not hidden from you, when I was being made in secret, intricately woven in the depths of the earth.

Your eyes saw my unformed substance; in your book were written, every one of them, the days that were formed for me, when as yet there was none of them.

I love one of the pillars of one of our local pregnancy centers in the area I live: "We do not look to the circumstances or events that led up to a child being conceived, but that a child has been conceived." A common rebuttal to this stance is instances where conception occurred by rape or incest. My heart and soul go out to women in those situations, and I have a heart to support them. The emotional pain from a violent and ungodly act is evil, and should be opposed, as our Lord opposes this sin. Though this child was conceived through rape, it is still a child. And even if this child brings to remembrance the evil events of that day, he or she is still a person made in God's image, and there are loving Christian homes where that child can experience the love of God despite the events surrounding his or her conception.

Imagine that this happens to a woman who loves Jesus, and she decides to keep the child because she loves Jesus. Despite the questions and confusion, nine months later she gives birth to a son. This son grows up in her home. As he grows, he sees in his mother a heart of love and compassion as she nurtures him physically and spiritually. She cuts his toenails. She reads him a story about Jesus before bed. She hugs, kisses, and cuddles him. Maybe she raises her son all by herself, and God provides for every need at every crossroad. Or maybe she has help: a mother, father, sibling, or grandparent who helps her along the way. Maybe she prays for a godly husband. Or maybe she doesn't, but God brings one to her anyway. Now this young child has a father too. Imagine he makes a profession of faith at a young age, and God stirs his spirit so much that he decides to go to Bible college, then seminary. He pastors a church, and God uses him throughout his life to foster a faithful ministry and to preach grace and repentance all of his days to a lost and dying world in the name of his faithful Savior Jesus. Regardless of the circumstances, Jesus Christ shows himself faithful to His promise to never leave her or forsake her.

If all of this were true and happened, could you say that the Spirit of God was not involved with this boy's conception? Could you say that because it was an evil act in which he was conceived, that therefore God was not the giver of his life, and that any blessings he experienced were chance coincidences? We must credit God for his wellbeing because God alone plans life. If we hold to the Word of God, that all of the days formed for us were written in God's book when yet there were none of them, we have to accept that God has a plan for everyone. (In this use in Scripture, "God's book" is not referring to the Bible, but to God's eternal decree and plan.) God was introduced to the situation even before the boy was conceived. We could never say, "*Without God, a life was brought forth.*" He was the Spirit that gave life for the conception. A woman who chooses to keep her child, even amidst the struggle, could adopt the words of David when he spared Saul's life: "*Behold, as your life was precious this day in my sight, so may my life be precious in the sight of the Lord, and may he deliver me out of all tribulation*" (I Samuel 26:24).

This takes faith. But if God works all things together for good for those who love Him, choosing life is included. We serve a God that provides for all of our needs. For reassurance of this, read Jesus' words about worrying in Matthew 6:25-34. He provides every time! He will give the crown of life to those who trust in Him. What are we living for and what do we view as the purpose of life? If we do not uphold life in the womb and *teach* that God will provide for that mother and her child, then we do not believe that God is more powerful and able than a mere man. We sin greatly, oh so greatly, when we do not preserve life.

Adam Rebandt

.

Chapter 5

Judah

Buried in the workings of a father who did not show equality to his sons, Judah spearheaded a life-saving event and showed that all of God's children are equally deserving of life. Judah was the fourth son of Jacob, who was also known as Israel. Jacob had two wives, Rachel and Leah. Rachel, mother of Joseph and Benjamin, was Jacob's favorite wife. But Judah's mother was Leah. Thus, Judah and Joseph were half-brothers. They had the same father but different mothers. (Genesis 37:3, ESV)

Israel loved Joseph more than his other sons because he was the child of his old age. He favored him, making him a robe of many colors. When his brothers saw that their father loved him more than them, they hated him and could not speak peacefully to him. Jacob did not love his sons with equality. Scripture does not try to hide this. Joseph's brothers hated and mistreated him because they were jealous of the favor their father gave Joseph.

Their resentment and hatred festered into a plot to kill their brother. Reuben, Joseph's older brother, initially thwarted the murder and instead suggested that they throw Joseph into a pit. But at some point, the oldest brother Reuben disappeared. The remaining brothers saw a caravan of Ishmaelites headed towards Egypt. Instead of killing Joseph, Judah spoke up for life. He said, "What profit is it if we kill our brother and conceal his blood? Come, let us sell him to the Ishmaelites, and let not our hand be upon him, for he is our brother, our own flesh" (Genesis 37:26, ESV).

Judah saved Joseph's life by persuading his brothers to sell Joseph. This may not have been the best possible solution; selling a brother into slavery is a serious sin. But murder is a final event that offers no change of course. A dead body is a dead body, an act of finality in this life. There is no going back. In his wisdom, Judah removed Joseph from his other brothers, so that he had a hope of survival. Slavery and murder are both sins with consequences. In this case, Joseph had hope and was ultimately delivered from slavery. There is no deliverance in this life from death, or a second chance. Judah did not want his brother handed over to final death. God will be the judge over each man's sins, be it slavery or murder.

After being sold into slavery, Joseph went on an incredible journey. He served in Potiphar's house, was thrown in prison for a crime he did not commit, interpreted dreams for Pharaoh, and was then made the second most powerful official in Egypt, behind only Pharaoh himself. What a path! He went from a near-death experience to being a leading official in Egypt. Joseph used his authority to help Egypt store food and thrive during a seven-year famine. The famine impacted the entire region, including Israel, where Joseph's family lived. The Bible says that ten of Joseph's brothers came to Egypt to purchase food. Benjamin, the youngest and son of Rachel, stayed home with Jacob. When they arrived, Joseph recognized them, but they did not recognize him. He accused his brothers of being spies, and to prove that they were not, he required them to bring Benjamin to Egypt. He put all the brothers in custody for three days, after which he decided to detain one brother while the rest returned to get Benjamin. The brothers then spoke in their native language, which Joseph understood, and talked about how much wrong they did him, not knowing it was him. Joseph bound Simeon and made him his prisoner, letting the rest of his brothers head home to their father Jacob. After explaining what happened to Simeon, Jacob refused to let Benjamin go back with them. He rejected Reuben's attempts to assure Jacob that he would bring Benjamin back, even when he offered the lives of his two grandsons as a guarantee that he would bring Benjamin home safely.

Judah had the opportunity to use his God-given gift of persuasiveness with words. Years earlier, he insisted that his brothers not kill Joseph, and "*his brothers listened to him*" (Genesis 37:27). It is important for us to speak on behalf of those who cannot speak, even with winsome words. It was Judah's words that compelled Joseph to reveal himself to his brothers, and it was Judah's words that eventually convinced Jacob that the brothers could take

Benjamin on the second journey to Egypt. But Judah was not perfect. His son Er was put to death because of wickedness, and he slept with his daughter-in-law Tamar. Tamar disguised herself as a prostitute, and Judah slept with her. He ended up leaving his signet, his cord, and his staff with her. Later, when Judah found out that Tamar was pregnant, his anger flared, and he ordered that she should be burned. Judah, a preserver of life, was ready to have her burned for the sin in which he had participated! He failed to understand the concept of equal standing, for he had committed the same sin as she, but believed that only she was worthy of death. As Tamar was brought out, she went up to her father-in-law and said she was made pregnant by the man to whom these items belonged. Then she brought out his signet, the cord, and the staff. When Judah saw this, he recalled his failure to give her to his son Shelah, saying, "She is more righteous than I, since I did not give her to my son Shelah." (Gen 38: 26).

Even when Judah was ready to take Tamar's life, God had already used him to preserve life. Perez, one of the twins resulting from their union, would become a direct ancestor of our living Savior Jesus. Judah's commitment to preserving Joseph's life foreshadowed the work of our Savior who is committed to preserving our life, and even Judah's initial failure to view Tamar with equal standing and defend her life reminds us that God is the ultimate giver and preserver of all life. We can be thankful for God's sovereignty! He often has great plans for those we fail to value; in this case it was Jesus, His greatest plan. Without Jesus, we are separated from God upon death, and our life is not preserved. It is lost forever. Our gracious Savior from the tribe of Judah preserves us, and then goes even further to give us an abundant life on earth and eternal life in heaven. He preserves us as a bride without blemish to present to His Heavenly Father. We have a picture in this scene of a father, a son, and a potential bride. Their failures provide a vivid contrast to our perfect heavenly Father. Judah admitted his unrighteousness and his failures as a father, while our heavenly Father is not only perfectly righteous but gave his Son to an unrighteous bride, you and me.

God does not need perfect people to accomplish His perfect plan because He is perfect. When Paul in the New Testament urges us to forget what is behind and to press on toward the goal, it is because we are imperfect. If we dwell on our sin, we feel useless. But when we look to Christ, we see perfection. The greatest joy I have every day is looking at Jesus: his perfection and his righteousness. He is wonderful to behold. I try not to focus on myself because there is not much to see. Let us fix our gaze on Christ so that we might become more like Him. Let us confess our sins and learn from our mistakes. The beauty of God's love exhibited through the gifting of his Son should make us leap for joy. This faith of equal standing that we have all obtained by the righteousness of our Lord and Savior Jesus Christ should compel us to press onward and not to dwell on the sins of the past. Did God bring Israel out of Egypt to return and die there? No. Likewise, Jesus has done the work for us. He is the giver of life. He has led us out of slavery to sin. If Jesus cares that much about life, should we not also?

Judah was persuasive. He knew how to convince someone to take action. The love of Christ compels and persuades us. Should we not present the love of Christ to the world so that they may also be persuaded by his love? Every Christian can ask God for boldness and eloquence (truth with love) to advocate for life. God has the power to save, so we must not be silent. Judah was also human. In his later life, his sin hindered him from recognizing Tamar's equal standing or imagining that God had a bigger plan. Let us learn from his mistakes and submit ourselves and our view of others to God's perfect authority.

Chapter 6

The Church Leaders – A Stance for Life

I have been in church and surrounded by church leaders for my entire life. My father has been the pastor of the same church for over 30 years. My uncle is a pastor. My grandfather is ordained and so is his brother. I have also visited many different churches throughout my life. As a child, my father would take us to a different church whenever he was not preaching. Even now, I visit new churches whenever I travel with my family. Over the years, I have noticed that a congregation tends to value what the leaders of the church value. Those leaders bear responsibility for the spiritual health of souls. As an elder myself, this is something of which I am always mindful.

We as church leaders must give an account for the people in our ministry. We are to be encouraging. We must gently instruct those who oppose us outside of Christ in the hope that God will grant them the repentance that leads to knowledge of the truth. There are many who do not have an understanding of God's truth because they are held captive by the devil, who leads them towards eternal damnation. This is a scary thought. But when we see a soul rescued from this captivity and brought to life, we rejoice all the more. It is in these moments that we as Christians see the power of God changing a life before our eyes. We realize that God's power does more than combat the lies and strongholds of the evil one; His power tears down those strongholds. As shepherds under the great Shepherd, we have been given the call to actively "save *others by snatching them out of the fire*" (Jude 23). God's power does the saving, but God uses us to shepherd His flock.

What does a shepherd do? A shepherd leads the sheep to green pastures, keeps the sheep on the path, and protects the sheep from predators. David is the best-known earthly shepherd in the Bible. 1 Samuel 17:34-35 says, *"But David said to Saul, 'Your servant used to keep sheep for his father. And when there came a lion, or a bear, and took a lamb from the flock, I went after him and struck him and delivered it out of his mouth. And if he arose against me, I caught him by his beard and struck him and killed him.'"*

The shepherd protects the lambs and the sheep, snatching them from their predators. When church leaders fail to shepherd, their sheep suffer. They get lost, hurt, and killed. A shepherd who fails to protect his vulnerable lambs essentially delivers them to their enemies. Church leaders who fail to discourage abortions are no different. They deliver the lamb into the lion's mouth. Jeremiah 1:5a says, *"Before I formed you in the womb I knew you, and before you were born I consecrated you."* God forms life. He knew us before we entered the womb. We must do everything in our power to deliver an unborn child from abortion, and we must speak out against abortion because it is such an injustice. Ezekiel 9 provides an example of God's response to those who defile life:

> *And the LORD said to him, "Pass through the city, through Jerusalem, and put a mark on the foreheads of the men who sigh and groan over all the abominations that are committed in it." And to the others he said in my hearing, "Pass through the city after him, and strike. Your eye shall not spare, and you shall show no pity. Kill old men outright, young men and maidens, little children and women, but touch no one on whom is the mark. And begin at my sanctuary." So they began with the elders who were before the house. Then he said to them, "Defile the house, and fill the courts with the slain. Go out." So, they went out and struck in the city. And while they were striking, and I was left alone, I fell upon my face, and cried, "Ah, Lord GOD! Will you destroy all the remnant of Israel in the outpouring of your wrath on Jerusalem?" Then he said to me, "The guilt of the house of Israel and Judah is exceedingly great. The land is full of blood, and*

the city full of injustice. For they say, 'The LORD has forsaken the land, and the LORD does not see.' As for me, my eye will not spare, nor will I have pity; I will bring their deeds upon their heads." And behold, the man clothed in linen, with the writing case at his waist, brought back word, saying, "I have done as you commanded me" (Ezekiel 9:5-11).

Like those in Ezekiel 9, we must "sigh and groan" over abominations in our world. The abominations in Ezekiel 9 are murder and rampant injustice. Abortion and racism are modern day equivalents. We must stand against these because all human life was made in the image of God and we all have equal standing before Him. God will bring wrath upon those who, actively or passively, take part in abominations against His people. The unborn are like lambs, and they must not simply be handed over to death. How the enemy has deceived many in authority.

When church leaders neglect to oppose injustice or racial inequality, they are refusing to view God's lambs with a faith of equal standing. This is a posture that I am unwilling to take. When I read Ezekiel 9, I am scared for any church leader who has ever supported or been indifferent to unjust practices, such as racism and abortion. How has the deceiver, the father of lies, really so misled any pastor or church leader into believing that a woman would be better off terminating her pregnancy? How can Christians believe this? It is inconsistent with the name Christ-ians. When we carry the name Christ, we must defend the lives for whom he died.

In Ezekiel 9, the man clothed in linen was asked to differentiate those who sigh and moan over the abominations of the land from those who were indifferent to or supportive of the abominations. God did not have pity on those who did not sigh and moan. We all know people today who are racist and pro-choice. They would not have been spared when the death angel passed through. Abortion is one form of racism. As sinful ideologies can keep us from God's mercy, we need to disassociate ourselves from our sinful thoughts.

Is it possible to shake our fists at God and ask why we see the problems that we do, when we as a land have done this to ourselves, and are still doing it?

When we as a church in America and across the globe are not unified in God's truth, God is not to blame. The church is responsible. In John 8:44, Jesus tells the religious leaders of his day, "*You are of your father the devil, and your will is to do your father's desires. He was a murderer from the beginning, and does not stand in the truth, because there is no truth in him. When he lies, he speaks out of his own character, for he is a liar and the father of lies.*"

The devil started lying to humans in the Garden of Eden, and he will continue to do so until Jesus Christ returns, and Satan is bound in Hell forever. Satan's lies lead to death, and he deceives us into killing the unborn. He is a murderer. He is The Murderer. When we see him as anything less, we do not understand our enemy. Satan's goal has always been to destroy us. He tempted us and led us to the physical death that entered the world through sin, and without Jesus we would all go to Hell and face eternal damnation forever. But in God's great plan of redemption, physical death does not mean spiritual death for those who have Jesus.

Satan desires to take as many as possible with him into death. Revelation 12:2-5 reiterates this:

> *She was pregnant and cried out in labor and agony as she was about to give birth. Then another sign appeared in heaven: There was a great fiery red dragon having seven heads and ten horns, and on its heads were seven crowns. Its tail swept away a third of the stars in heaven and hurled them to the earth. And the dragon stood in front of the woman who was about to give birth, so that when she did give birth it might devour her child. She gave birth to a Son, a male who is going to rule all nations with an iron rod. Her child was caught up to God and to his throne.*

Satan sought to devour Him who would rule all nations. This is none other than Jesus. Satan thought he had won when Jesus died on the cross, but he did not anticipate Jesus rising again from the dead in His own power. How Satan must rejoice with every death by abortion! Abortion facilities are chambers of death where people embrace ease and comfort and forsake the God of life. But Jesus came that we might have life and have it abundantly.

I fear for those who preach in the name of Jesus Christ and do not moan and groan over the abominations committed in our land. Through God's Holy Spirit, sinners are called to repent. My prayer is that leaders in the church who have erred will immediately repent and seek forgiveness. Their lives still matter to God, despite their past sins, and God will forgive them.

Adam Rebandt

Chapter 7

Equal Opportunity Evangelism

The book of Matthew ends with these words of Jesus: "*Go therefore and make disciples of all nations, baptizing them in the name of the Father and of the Son and of the Holy Spirit, teaching them to observe all that I have commanded you. And behold, I am with you always, to the end of the age* (Matthew 28:19-20). This faith of equal standing is a result of God's Sovereignty. We were called to receive His Light and to extend this light to the world. We are to be a city on a hill that cannot be hidden.

Jesus tells us to be salt and light in the world. Both salt and light change their environment. Salt gives flavor to food and, in the right amounts, makes that food more desirable to eat. In Jesus' day, salt wasn't just a flavoring; it actually preserved meat. If our society is to be preserved, it will be through the church reaching into culture. Light penetrates the darkness and allows us to see clearly. We are to be that light that leads people out of the darkness to Jesus by His Holy Spirit. We need to look at our faith as a faith of equal opportunity. We need to share it freely. It is God who saves, and we must not be selective with whom we share the Gospel. We cannot predict a person's coming to salvation based upon their lifestyle, background, or heritage. To do so is to misunderstand the changing power of God on lives and to deny that *we* would be on the road to destruction if God did not save us. Our preconceived expectations have nothing to do with what God will do, and He often completes works that we thought impossible.

We may have various reasons for neglecting to witness to those around us, but one in particular is worth examining. Even after being saved, we may not have a full understanding of what we have been saved from or an awareness of our complete depravity before the Holy God. In other words, we are too satisfied with being saved, and lack a holy zeal to go into all the world, make disciples of Jesus, and see people rescued. Perhaps our faith seems too mundane to share. This is just not true! If we regularly consider how we have been rescued by God, our hearts should be so full of gratitude that we are unashamed to speak of Him in public. We become empowered by His promise to be with us always. We do not fear ridicule and rejection. We have such a love for every fellow human that we make it our mission to show others what God has done for us.

The source of the problem may be a disconnect from God's Word. Perhaps we are not rooted in Scripture to the point of acting in obedience. We might instead be focused on obtaining ease and comfort. But these worldly treasures are false idols. The deceiver dangles them in front of us. He wants to lead unbelievers into a spiritual death where there is only separation from God. And for believers, he wants to take away our effectiveness, distract us with the cares of this life, and diminish our opportunities and desire to spread the light.

Adjusting how we spend our time can help rectify this disconnect. As Christians, we need to evaluate where we put our energy. God alone is the agent of change. Ask Him to change you. How great would it be if our hobbies were loving Jesus, reading His Word, and praying? Maybe we just need to wake up earlier so that we have time to meet with Him and learn from His Word. When we pursue Jesus, the world will notice. They will see that we do not pursue the things that they deem to be treasures. The world will be blinded by the light of Christ, and the real Treasure will be seen in us.

How we handle the obstacles in our life can be an effective tool of evangelism. Christians should rely on Christ at every turn. We should handle change, frustrations, and difficulties with grace. When we are anchored in Christ, the storms of life will not move us. This can have a powerful impact on those around us. They will see our confidence in Christ and be drawn to it.

The Christian should also consistently embody an attitude of thankfulness. We should be content in our present circumstances and even give thanks for them. We must keep in mind that spiritual blessing is more important than physical blessing. Knowing Christ is a spiritual blessing that lasts for eternity. Physical blessing is material. It fades. *"What does it profit a man to gain the whole world but forfeit his own soul?*" (Mark 8:36). Christians truly begin to live for Christ when they are ready to die for Him and to themselves. In this, we find complete freedom to pursue Christ above all else. This produces a contagious evangelism. It comes through practice and by the constant use of His Word in our lives.

If we ask Him, God will give us greater confidence. At the store the other day, I overheard a woman telling a salesperson about her upcoming trip to Israel. I assumed that she was planning to see the biblical sites, and she was. But when I asked her about it, she was almost ashamed to admit it in public. I too have been there, lacking the confidence that we should already have because of the Holy Spirit living in us. We are to encourage the timid. Despite some discomfort, we should never be afraid to speak the spiritual truths, of greater worth than pure gold, and to speak up. The church is a large army, and we are not alone. If we really believe that our faith is something worth having and that it is the difference between death and life, we should be willing to share it. If we are not, then we may need to ask God to help us have the compassion of Jesus for the lost. This compassion will drive our desire to share Jesus with them.

It can be difficult to turn an average conversation into a spiritual one. I like to ask the simple question: "What *has your relationship with God been throughout your life?*" There is usually a pause, but a response almost always follows. I had one man tell me that he had never really thought about it, but even this gave me an opportunity to talk with him. Anything that opens the door to a spiritual conversation has potential. Not everyone is receptive, but many are. I also like to ask if there is anything that I can pray for. Their response provides a window into their life and their struggles. But more importantly, it creates an opportunity for God to show up in their life by answering their prayer. You may recall in Acts 10 that Cornelius prayed to God before he even became a Christian, and God told Cornelius that his prayer had been heard.

Evangelism is a process. It is not something we do once. It is most effective in relationships. I believe that every Christian should have non-Christian friends, and that we should be concerned if we do not. Jesus dined with tax collectors and sinners. Let us realize that we are the light of the world. We are not to discriminate when we share the good news. Sometimes God surprises us. When our church began in 1987, we did a mass mailing in Farmington Hills, Michigan. My father, a young pastor at the time, was one of those selecting names for the mailing list. He came to one name and thought that this one person would never come, so he did not address an envelope to him. Apparently, someone else did, because of all the letters sent, the man who received this letter was the only person who showed up. God called him from death to life, and he joined the family of Jesus. God can call anybody. He called Saul, the worst of sinners. Let us do our part, evangelizing all, and allow God's power to do the rest. He knows what He is doing.

Chapter 8

Music –
Faith of Equal Standing?

God wants worshipers. He desires to be glorified and lifted high among His people. One way we do this is by singing and playing musical instruments. I love singing hymns, psalms, and spiritual songs. I love singing to the Lord a new song. The act of singing to God puts gratitude in my heart for Him.

Music, however, can divide the church. Any aspect of worship can offend someone, for as Paul says, "*when I desire to do good, I find it to be a law that evil is right alongside*" (Romans 7:21). Churches and leaders and congregants may disagree about which instruments are appropriate for worship. Many churches esteem the piano, which isn't even mentioned in the Word of God. The Bible mentions the lyre and the flute and the harp, and refers to David's dancing as an act of worship, but how many churches integrate these things into their services? God's Word tells us to "*address… one another in psalms and hymns and spiritual songs, singing and making melody to the Lord with [our] hearts[s]*" and to "*praise Him with sounding cymbals… with loud clashing cymbals*" (Ephesians 5:19, Psalms 150:5, ESV). If God has prescribed it, then He accepts it. Bring out the percussion and wind instruments and dancing! Our view of acceptable worship may reveal how well we grasp the notion of equal standing. The enemy knows that music can be divisive, and he uses it to his advantage. Through a careful study of God's Word, we must answer the question, "*what has God said about worship?*" then align our hearts with His answer. All instruments and melodies are appropriate for worshiping our Savior when used in joyful reverence and with a heart of worship. Even some of the tunes that David used in the Psalms were taken from neighboring countries.

In assessing the legitimacy of our musical worship, we must ask whether it pleases God and whether it edifies others. We are not there for ourselves but to worship God. When something is not acceptable to God, it doesn't matter whether or not it makes someone feel good. Sometimes styles of worship feel uncomfortable and do not appear to edify or encourage others because they don't conform to a prescribed mold. But if God is honored, then perhaps we need to question whether our understanding of propriety in worship comes from God's Word or from our own history or culture. Each person, standing on holy ground, must "*remove his shoes*" and gaze at what God has said about worship. Once we know that something pleases God, it becomes easier to view that thing properly and be encouraged by it, even if we had previously forfeited some joy by not knowing fully what pleased God and what He accepted.

I have come to enjoy worshiping God however I can, with or without instruments, in singing hymns or praise songs. The style does not matter because worship is not about me. It is about God. If we believe that all Christians have a faith of equal standing, we must have a bigger picture of all that God accepts, rather than a narrow view of what we like or what makes us most comfortable. Things like the volume and pace of music only become problems when I am focused on myself. Preferences are fine, but we are called to worship God with others who are also in obedience. Problems arise when we substitute our preference for God's preference. God wants hearts of praise. Some worship Christ with the old hymns of the faith; others worship Christ with an electric guitar or rap music. Rap music is not of the devil, as some might think. It can be a wonderful tool for memorizing His Word with song and hiding His Word in our heart, that we might not sin against Him (Psalm 199:11).

Sometimes we feel like others need to adapt to our preferences, and that they are spiritually inferior because they do not worship God how He wants. But what does God want? He is concerned with the heart (spirit) and theology (truth). If our worship lacks spirit, we are not worshiping God the way He desires. If our worship lacks truth, we are not worshipping God the way that He desires. As we mature in the faith, we realize that our preferences are not that important. We can be content praising God in a cornfield or with brothers and sisters at church, as long as it is done in spirit and truth.

If we want to keep our young people in the church, we might consider incorporating into worship any of their musical preferences which God also accepts. We all want to see young people walking in the truth. But in America, we see a generation that does not prioritize the worship of God. Of course, we worship God at all moments and with every breath, and do not turn it on or off. But in this context, I refer to time set aside solely for the worship of God with others. The Bible warns us against "*neglecting to meet together, as some people do,*" but tells us to "*encourage one another, and all the more as you see the Day approaching*" (Hebrews 10:25). Some young people set an example for all believers, but many of the young people we desperately want to keep in church are babes in the faith and must stay in church for their faith to take root. Jesus wants them near him: "*Let the little children come to me, and do not hinder them, for to such belongs the kingdom of heaven*" (Matthew 19:14, ESV).

We should want our music to excite our young people about God and about worshiping Him. While there always has to be a reverence and respect for God, we must be cautious about labeling new music irreverent. If God is not uncomfortable with it, but we are, we cannot conflate our discomfort with God's displeasure. What is fine in the car is fine during Sunday morning worship in the church setting. Many in today's church would feel profoundly uncomfortable worshiping in the manner of the Old Testament. Imagine: loud clapping, drums, dancing with all of your might, shouting with loud SHOUTS of joy. There are churches that accept the full range of God's definition of worship; however, there are many others that restrict His definition. Our corporate worship should demonstrate our acceptance of God's definition of worship and our understanding that God has created instruments for His glory, hymns for His glory, and even tempo for His glory, as suggested in Psalm 150. Everyone has preferences, but when our preferences and God's definition conflict, we need to align our thoughts to His. Whether we worship individually unto God or corporately unto God, it must proceed from our hearts and minds towards what God says and accepts.

A greater openness to unfamiliar forms of worship might help others along and bring the joy that comes from seeing our children walking in the truth. When we understand our faith of equal standing, no preference is holier than another. If a style of music might help others grow, let's humble ourselves for the sake of those who may not be as strong in the faith as we are. At a meet and greet several months ago, a well-known national speaker and author said that the church she goes to has loud music that appeals to the young people. She knows that the music honors God, and said that when it gets too loud, she just puts in her ear plugs and still worships, for the sound still comes through! She just loves seeing the young people in church hearing the Word of God and excited to be there. We are living in a time when fewer and fewer of the next generation are in church regularly. The church in America is hardly being flooded with people lining up to come in, and yet we have the most joyful opportunity set before us and the whole world. If God accepts it in His definition, we just need to redefine ours. When we see others rejoicing in His Name, we can have a joy of our own. Variety is wonderful!

Chapter 9

White and Black – Spiders and Puke You Didn't Know Was There

Often, we do not understand a brother or sister's viewpoint because we don't understand the situations experienced by them or those close to them. A white person hasn't been on the receiving end of the terrible sentiment that some white people had and still have towards black people. Our eyes, ears, and heart can begin to interpret and understand others, but this understanding can never be based on experience.

My wife Sarah is terrified of spiders. She is a tough mom of six and remains calm in just about every circumstance. But if a spider is nearby, it is like death itself has entered the room. Early in our marriage, we lived in Australia for a few months, and some of the spiders there are the size of dinner plates. They make a sound when they jump in the water. Their legs click on the floor when they run. One night she was startled by a spider on the door of our house. She grabbed my arm tightly as she froze in place. I removed it by shooing it off, but neglected to kill it. I could have gone after it with the manly protective vengeance of a shining knight, but my strength did not come through. She describes my effort as lackluster because I failed to get rid of the problem and because my shooing was more like a limp fish waving at the spider than a strong attack. To this day, my paltry effort has remained an example of subpar management. Another time, Sarah was having a Bible study with a group of Australian women, and a spider, actually the size of a small dinner plate, ran across the floor. The Australian women ignored it, but my wife was horrified, to say the least. When the other ladies saw her reaction, the woman whose home they were meeting in said *"Yaw, I sar it in the shower this morning. I shooed it out of the tub with my broom."* WHAT?! To Sarah, it was incomprehensible that someone would knowingly remain in the same house with such a monster.

Spiders can be both good and evil, as it were, but if you have only experienced fear and terror, you will not understand or see that they can also have good and redeeming purposes. An African slave with a demeaning and harsh master in the early days of our country might not believe that a white person could have any good in him. If you grew up without any negative experiences, then your mind will reach different conclusions. Take a look at both sides. Spiders can be scary. Poisonous spiders like the black widow or redback can kill you. However, spiders also provide important benefits. They are natural pesticides. They kill off other insects that would otherwise cause serious harm to humanity. Their role in the ecosystem allows us to live longer and healthier lives.

The spider illustration may provide an analogy for many black Americans' perceptions of white people. Stories from firsthand experience, passed down through the generations, create perspective. This has caused separation. Sinful actions always have consequences, and we must work through them to the better side: God's side. It is understandable; some white people have been a serious threat to some blacks throughout the history of our nation. They defied dignity and taught that certain men and women were not fully human and deserving of the same God-given equal rights. Black Americans were terrorized, hung at the gallows, separated from their families, beaten, falsely accused, imprisoned, denied equal rights on buses and bathrooms, required to use separate drinking fountains, and much more. As a white man, I speak with deep sorrow and sadness about past and present racially charged atrocities. Black people were slaves to white people in America. Given this, it is ironic that we call it the land of the free and the home of the brave. But on the good and upright side, there were some white people who vehemently opposed slavery by speaking and preaching against it, helping to free slaves, and even fighting against it to the point of death.

If you are a black American with a family history that includes any of the injustices done in the past by some of the white race, then you will likely have a hard time trusting a white person. Can anyone really blame you? Similarly, it would probably take years of counseling for my wife to appreciate the redeeming qualities of a spider. She does not trust them. All that she knows is fear. If you are not a black American, then you cannot imagine the obstacles that some have had to overcome to believe God's truth that complete healing is not only possible but is what we are called to do. Consider some examples that took place on the very soil we call home.

The dark part of our history can be seen even from a pulpit. Here is an excerpt from an eighteenth-century sermon that a bishop of Virginia gave to slaves: "*Almighty God hath been pleased to make you slaves here and give you nothing but labour and poverty in this world, which you are obliged to submit to as it is His will that it should be so. Your bodies, you know, are not your own: they are at the disposal of those who you belong to*" (Chambers, William - American Slavery and Colour, 1857, page 143). When I read this, I immediately think, "*Remove the false teacher, who breathes lies, and does not understand the Gospel or Jesus who came to redeem.*" Our bodies do not belong to any other but the Lord Jesus. He has purchased us with His blood. It is horrific to think that some proud fallen "preacher" would preach that black bodies belong to another human. What an evil work this was. Satan was behind this, not God, but we are still each responsible for our sins. All bodies and souls belong to God.

We must shout to drown out the voice of the false one. Silence is not an option. We can do this with boldness, knowing we have the truth about equality given us in the infallible Word of God, from the great I AM Himself. The image of God is imprinted on all life the moment God brings it into existence in the womb of a woman. We must oppose the father of lies with truth and boldness, knowing that his arguments are futile because they oppose God's Word. Nowhere does the Bible teach that one person can own another. Rather, Jesus died so that we could all belong to God. Only the sacrifice of Jesus is sufficient to cover the sins of any man. He became a servant for us, giving up His body for us. Understanding that we all belong equally to God and have equal standing before Him should eliminate racial prejudice. We belong to God, and because we belong to God, we are willing to serve our brothers and sisters and give ourselves up for them, the same way Christ did for the church.

The nineteenth-century bishop trampled on the Word of God and elevated himself above God. Are we too blind to see the lasting impacts of this kind of sin? Although this happened generations ago, it had an impact that in some families is still being felt today. We must stop elevating ourselves over God's Name and God's Word. Are we afraid to ask God to show us His wisdom? Are we afraid to read His Word and find truth that might call us to change our ways and conform to His will? If we are His children, why would we want anything but His way?

Unfortunately, this sermon was not an isolated incident. There were countless examples of injustice throughout the slavery years of our country and there are still examples in modern times. Human trafficking, manipulation of people, slavery, abortion, and class systems still exist in our world, and are evidence that we don't understand equal standing. These things are a slap in the face of the Creator who gives us every breath we breathe.

The nineteenth-century bishop lacked wisdom. His teaching opposed God's Word because he considered himself better than others. That mocks God. We need to discard all false teaching no matter where it comes from. Reading God's Word allows us to hear His voice and to discard anything antithetical to it. Being rooted in His Word provides a boldness to speak out against the teachings and voices of the enemy. We have the confidence of the Holy Spirit in our being, leading us forward. He who leads us into each battle is the One who conquers every enemy. The following examples display a mindset opposed to God and to the notion of equal standing:

The first comes from Solomon Northup's "Twelve Years a Slave," written in 1854:

An hour before daylight the horn is blown. Then the slaves arouse, prepare their breakfast, fill a gourd with water, in another, deposit their dinner of cold bacon and corn cake, and hurry to the field again.

It is an offense invariably followed by a flogging to be found at the quarters after daybreak. Then the fears and labours of another day begin and until its close there is no such thing as rest ... with the exception of ten or fifteen minutes, which is given them at noon to swallow their allowance of cold bacon, they are not permitted to be a moment idle until it is too dark to see, and when the moon is full, they oftentimes labour till the middle of the night. They do not dare to stop even for dinner time, nor return to the quarters, however late it be, until the order to halt is given by the driver.

Or consider this newspaper advertisement from the New Orleans Bee, quoted by William Goodell in <u>American Slave Code in Theory and Practice</u>: *"NEGROES FOR SALE – A negro woman, twenty-four years of age, and her two children, one eight and the other three years old. Said negroes will be sold SEPARATELY or together as desired. The woman is a good seamstress. She will be sold low for cash, or EXCHANGED FOR GROCERIES. For terms, apply to Matthew Bliss & CO., 1 Front Levee"* What about the desires of the mother and her children? Was Dad already ripped from the family and sold separately?

John G. Fee, of Berea, Kentucky, was one of the leading abolitionists of his day, and I highly recommend his autobiography. He was born to a slave owner and faithfully studied and adhered to God's Word. In his autobiography he tells his wife, "*I cannot redeem all slaves, nor even all in my father's family, but the labors of Julett and her husband contributed in part to the purchase of the land I yet own in Indiana, and to sell those lands and redeem her will be in some measure returning to her and her husband what they have toiled.*" Sadly, despite John's efforts, Julett, her husband, and their children were not able to be a family. Julett and her husband had been separated earlier and were never to reunite again. A family is an institution set up by God. God weeps when families are separated. He wept when families were broken apart by slavery. God has called us to always gaze on His presence.

While there are many stories of abuse of black slaves in America at the hands of white people, there were also white people who, like John Fee, worked to free the slaves. These slaves had a story to tell of how a white family helped emancipate them. There are even modern day stories of how white Americans have reached out and assisted black Americans to get a head start. Star Parker is one example; another is Dr. Carol Swain, former professor at Vanderbilt University.

We inherited sin from the first Adam, and we now find ourselves in the midst of a battle against it everywhere. Ephesians 6:12 says, "*we do not wrestle against flesh and blood, but against the rulers, against the authorities, against the cosmic powers over this present darkness, against the spiritual forces of evil in the heavenly places.*" When we look at our history and at the issues of our day, we realize what sheep we are! We are sheep who go astray and lack any ability to guide or lead on our own. The bishop lacked wisdom and truth. He needed to be taught by the Great Shepherd in order to properly shepherd his hearers. Psalm 138:2 elevates God's name and His Word above all else: "*I bow down toward your holy temple and give thanks to your name for your steadfast love and your faithfulness, for you have exalted above all things your name and your word*" (ESV).

Thankfully, we cannot spend time in God's presence, meditate on His Word, follow Him, and not be changed. We must open up our hearts and desire to have Him align our mindset with His. When we learn to hear the Shepherd's voice, we can recognize Satan's lies. Spending time with Him is different than just thinking about spending time with Him. We must be in His presence. When we do, we see truth clearly. It is not hidden.

If I am honest, the most exciting part of my life is time alone with the Triune God. I look forward to it more than anything else, I long for it more than anything else, and when I miss it for any reason, I long for it again. My Jesus and His Word is the well that never runs dry. God is always in His Word, teaching an open heart. It is important to spend time with God, but He has not called us to be in quiet for our whole existence, and uninvolved with people. He has called us to learn and pray in quiet and to be highly involved in serving Him by serving others the rest of our time. This too is an act of worship. You are my ministry. I am your ministry. God has called us to go into all the world and make disciples. He has called us to be active in the world around us, and he leads us with His truth.

When we have consistent time with Him each day, His Word accomplishes in us a desire to reach out to others. This is the source of strength. The strength that we receive from Him changes us and allows us to be bold and to speak up for those who cannot speak for themselves. Fellowship with Him changes our focus. We have a responsibility to respond to the evils that have been done in history and which continue to persist. You were chosen for this season and time. You are in the puke, even if you did not ask for it. The history of spiders exists, and you are in the puke. We are here now, living in the midst of this land, today.

When Sarah and I were newly married and still in Australia, we went to the Great Barrier Reef. It was a long drive north along the east coast of Australia to Airlie Beach. From Airlie Beach, it is a two-hour boat ride to the reef. The first 30-45 minutes were in the inland channels where the water was calm. During this time, they showed a movie and offered signup for a guided snorkeling tour that would occur once we disembarked the ship upon reaching the reef. We signed up, not wanting to miss this rare opportunity. When we left the inland channels and headed into the open ocean, the water became choppy. It was still safe, but certainly unsettling for those with motion sensitivities like Sarah. I noticed her discomfort but was fixated on the movie. Finally, Sarah nudged me and said, "*I am really not feeling well; I need to go find a restroom.*" There was not much I could do at that point to help her, so I said OKAY and hoped that she would feel better. She got up and headed to the bathroom, and I stayed watching the coral reef, sea creatures, and God's beauty. As I watched and watched, I forgot that Sarah was not watching until a half hour or so had passed. All of a sudden it occurred to me that she was not back yet, and I became worried. I went and found a woman and asked her to check the women's bathroom to see if Sarah was in there. Sarah was in the bathroom, but she was so sick that she could not respond when the woman called for her. The woman came out and told me that she did not find anyone in there. I asked her to try again. She did and found Sarah this time. Not only was Sarah violently ill, but she had also developed a migraine. She was stuck on the ship with nowhere to go and no way to get help. I tried to console her, but I could not make her feel better. Knowing that the guided tour would start as soon as we got off the ship, I told Sarah that I was fine canceling the tour, no matter the cost. I just wanted her to be okay; the snorkeling did not matter that much. But she insisted that we go since we had paid the money. I tried several times to dissuade her, but her mind was made up. We were going snorkeling.

If I may stop right here and say thank you to God for creating women, especially my woman. There is another level of strength, focus, and endurance that my wife has that I simply do not. She amazed me that day, and she has every day since. What an amazing gift to man is woman!

We finally arrived and docked the ship in the middle of the ocean but had no time to rest in a fixed spot, as our snorkeling adventure was ready to begin. Sarah was still feeling horrible, and I had no idea how she would survive this. We geared up and entered the water as a group. The guide said, "*get used to the water and get your snorkeling gear, and then we will start the tour*." So we did, and it was amazing. We could see all the way down to the bottom. And then, it happened. The moment I will never forget. I remember it like it was yesterday.

Sarah tapped me on the shoulder and said, "*I'm going to have to…*" Then the puke flew. There it was, and there it went, right in front of us and into the ocean. I turned to my right and there was my man, completely unaware of what awaited him, snorkeling right towards the orange glob of puke. He swam right into it. When he came up, he looked right at us. His hair and goggles were covered in vomit. I gave him a very normal what's-up nod, hesitant to draw attention to the situation. He went back under and got a nice fresh saltwater cleaning.

Like this unsuspecting snorkeler, those of us living in America today did not know what we were entering. We didn't choose the country or time or family we would be born into. We have inherited cultural tensions that impact relationships between whites and blacks. But we can still have hope. God is always ahead of us. He is Sovereign and therefore in control. As my dad once paraphrased Ephesians 1:11: "*God has absolute rule, reign, and authority over all of His creation in such a way and so much so that He has foreordained whatsoever comes to pass for the praise of His glory*." Much like the unsuspecting snorkeler, we are swimming in someone else's mess. However, God is still in control, and He works out all things for the good of His people. A person with white skin cannot just say *"that was the past, and that's it. All is good now."* All is not good now. In fact, often well-meaning folks find themselves in the puke, that is, in the results of something that was nasty before they got there. We owe it to every black person in our country to listen to their story, to stand up for their values, to understand them, and to serve them. This is what the body of Christ does....it just happens that the issue that was there before us all was a black/white issue. It should be second nature to let a black person go in front of us in a line or if we arrive at a door at the same time, because that is just what the body of Christ does. There are many black people who, with the kindness of humanity, will let a white person go first, because that is what the body of Christ does. Always take the lead with kindness, for this is what Christ expects of us. And it may not hurt to take extra steps of kindness towards those who have been mistreated. We cannot undo the past, but we are called to love in the present. Our nation is in a precarious place, and we should lead with an unhesitating and loving heart because we are equal.

There is no such thing as a partial human. To be created in God's image makes us all equal and fully human in God's sight. As a follower of Jesus, I need to do something about the inequality that persists today. Racial conflict is one way the devil uses comparison to disrupt every sphere of human relationships. We need to view other people as equal, and proactively embody this belief. In Christ we have an equal standing; let us demonstrate this truth to the world around us.

When we do this, we disarm the devil's use of comparison. I remember having coffee with a fellow brother in the faith. We are in a similar line of work, so it would have been easy for us to compare ourselves to one another. It can be tempting to think of someone else as better or worse because of what they have or do not have. But this way of thinking distracts us from what God has called us to do. Why are we comparing ourselves to other people? Let us measure our lives by the life of Jesus, and try to be more like Him. I had to be conscious of wholeheartedly viewing my friend as a brother of equal standing, for we both have faith in Christ and are living for Him.

One way to move towards relationships that view one another with equal importance is to be proactive in our words and actions. I go as far as to say *"How is my brother (or sister) of equal standing doing today?"* We also show equality by associating with all people. Who do I spend time with? Who do I hang out with? Who do I sit next to? Who do I invite into my home? When we greet each other as a brother and sister of equal standing and spend time with all people, it transforms the view that we have of all people. Knowing that we have an equal faith, we should humbly treat others better than ourselves and be willing to serve one another.

God is proactive. He reaches out to us before we reach out to Him. A simple hello may open the door to a new God-ordained friendship. When we open our mouth in public to confront or challenge inequality, we honor the Lord by seeking truth and encouraging those around us to speak with love. Jesus told the deaf man, *"Be opened!"* when he opened His ears. I would challenge you to do the same. Pray for God's wisdom and be open-minded to what He says.

Chapter 10

Black and White – Confronting our Legacy from Different Perspectives

In 1808, our country abolished the international slave trade. Although we prohibited importing slaves from Africa and elsewhere, we did not abolish slavery. We still allowed and supported the domestic "breeding" and sale of slaves until slavery was abolished in 1865. Between 1808 and 1865, over half of enslaved families were separated, and most were never reunited. Our country not only failed its mission to unite all people under a banner of independence; it actively dismembered families. Imagine a daughter who sees her father sold from one slave owner to another. She would carry those emotional scars for the rest of her life. Leaders in our country's heritage allowed this to happen. They did not speak up for those who could not speak for themselves. Proverbs 31:8–9, says "*Speak up for those who cannot speak for themselves, for the rights of all who are destitute. Speak up and judge fairly; defend the rights of the poor and needy.*" Collectively, our nation failed to do this.

We may point our finger at the slave owners and slave traders, but slavery was legal. Where was the voice of reason? There were clearly unqualified people in positions of power with ungodly views that rendered them unable to make godly decisions. We need leaders in every sphere who can make God-honoring decisions. Why don't we just get on the side of God? Who do we think we are? Humans are created by God, and He has told us how to live. God promises us that "*for those who love God all things work together for good, for those who are called according to his purpose*" (Romans 8:28). Not once in human history has someone honored God's Word and had it worked out for evil. It may have appeared so, but we can be confident that God worked it for good. God's Word always functions at 100%, working things together for good and for His glory. Even our suffering, or the apparent evil in our lives, is not worthy to be compared with that which will be revealed to us. God's Word has never missed an opportunity to use all things to work together for good; it never returns void. It has always accomplished the purposes that He has for it. What is the percentage for human words? I would rather not talk about it. Our lives are a vapor. We are going to see our Savior soon, so let's follow His path. We will find out that His Word has never failed, so let's live life now as though His Word never fails. Human wisdom leads to destruction. Immoral laws tear families apart.

My father will tell you that family makes a difference. He has been a pastor for thirty years and has seen the many ways that family makes a difference. He has sat on crime prevention committees with different police chiefs. He has served as a chaplain in the FBI-NA. He has dealt with situations in the community because of his positions, and there is a strong correlation between how a family raises a child and how that child turns out. When one family member turns to Christ, that family now has a built-in preacher to tell the rest of the family the great works that God has done. God's Word shows God's faithfulness to a thousand generations of those who love Him and keep His commandments. In ministry, my father has seen that God's Word does not return void in families. It is a cord throughout Scripture. The family is one of the clearest paths that God uses to grow His kingdom. Broken families lead to lingering spiritual and functional consequences. He works through all situations, but we must understand exactly what He intended for families.

The ideology that created this mess in our country is, like all sin, diametrically opposed to Christ. For us to fulfill the Great Commission, we must understand equal standing, viewing everyone as important and worth reaching with the Gospel and as worthy of being a part of our fellowship. The following extended excerpt from an article provides an example of how God used humility to His Word to bring back unity, knowledge, and wisdom to Bob Jones University in South Carolina:

> *A fundamentalist Christian University has apologized for racist policies including a one-time ban on interracial dating that wasn't lifted until nine years ago and its unwillingness to admit black students until 1971.*
>
> *Bob Jones University founded in 1927 in South Carolina said its rules on race were shaped by culture instead of the Bible, according to a statement posted Thursday on its Web site.*
>
> *The university, with about 5,000 students, didn't begin admitting black students until nearly 20 years after the U.S. Supreme Court's 1954 Brown v. Board of Education ruling found public segregated schools were unconstitutional.*
>
> *"We failed to accurately represent the Lord and to fulfill the commandment to love others as ourselves. For these failures we are profoundly sorry. Though no known antagonism toward minorities or expressions of racism on a personal level have ever been tolerated on our campus, we allowed institutional policies to remain in place that were racially hurtful," the statement said.*
>
> *The interracial dating ban was lifted in March 2000, not long after the policy became an issue in the Republican presidential primary. Then-candidate George W. Bush was criticized when he spoke at the school during one of his first campaign stops.*
>
> *Bob Jones University President Stephen Jones decided to issue the apology because the school still receives questions about its views on race.*
>
> *The leader of the South Carolina National Association for the Advancement of Colored People said the civil rights group welcomed the statement.*

"It's unfortunate it took them this long — particularly a religious, faith-based institution — to realize that we all are human beings and the rights of all people should be respected and honored," said Lonnie Randolph, president of the association's state chapter.

Randolph said that when Jones became president three years ago, he asked the civil rights leader not to hold the decisions made under his father and grandfather against him.

Jones is the great-grandson of the school founder, Bob Jones. He took over for his father, also named Bob Jones, in 2005 (Associated Press - updated 11/21/2008 4:07:46 PM ET Print Font: nbcnew.com).

The university said that "*its rules on race were shaped by culture instead of the Bible*" and admitted that they "*failed to accurately represent the Lord and to fulfill the commandment to love others as ourselves.*" True repentance should always follow genuine apology. This includes a forsaking of the past sin, not to repeat it, and a turning to follow Christ with obedience from that point forward. American institutions and individuals have hurt black people, even if individually you believe you have not. Remember, you are in the puke. If I am truly sorry that you are hurting, I will apologize without you seeking it. You may be the loving spider, but to certain populations of black people you have only been known as the harmful one. It is their position that you should be concerned with, not yours. If you do not hold any prejudice in your heart, by God's grace and for His glory, Amen, let me appreciate you, but there may still be work ahead of you. Being a person created in God's image and also with emotions, I can hate my sin when I realize I have offended you, then proactively seek forgiveness and work at changing my behavior. Even when it isn't us who committed the sin, we must realize that we wear a skin color that associates us with certain ideologies and actions. We must be gentle. God will give us whatever credit we deserve, rendering to each one according to what he or she has done, and at the end, we will realize the only credit that saves us is that of Christ's perfect life in our place, His righteousness, given to us. I am called by God to do the right thing, following Christ, regardless of how I am perceived, and to do right regardless of the response. The result we long for is not always immediate. If I have offended my wife, for example, it may take time for her to believe I have changed. As I take initiative and verbalize my apology while demonstrating changed actions, even multiple times for the same offense, our relationship improves. Indifference shows a lack of care. When white people are indifferent to the offenses that our race has caused, it communicates that we don't care. Therein lies much of the problem. God calls us to care, and we must. I admire Stephen Jones' apology because it was grounded in the Word. His willingness to state that his family and school espoused views counter to the teaching of the Bible was important. We must be truly repentant, realizing that the effort needs to be initiated on our end and not ignored. Once reconciliation occurs in Christ, a relationship is restored. There is no reason to harbor any condemnation. At this point, the Word of God was useful for correction. If it does one of its intended purposes, to correct, should we not just rejoice that correction has taken place and that God's Word is proved true yet again? Now, we must live in harmony.

Another way the church errs is with tradition. Tradition can have its place if it is based upon the Word of God. But we must value the teachings of the Bible over our tradition. A church leader once told a pastor friend of mine, "*I suppose that we have followed our tradition, whereas you have followed the Word of God.*" When we make a decision apart from the Word of God, we fail. This example was taken from a church that holds largely to the doctrines of man and tradition and has admittedly held the Word of God subservient to man's traditions. This is an example of what we are NOT to do. We must confront the legacy of our past and even our traditions, so that we can unveil past flaws that linger.

As white people, we often dismiss the flawed legacies of slavery and racism in our families and nation, because we personally do not support or advocate such evil practices. Let us accept and admit that there are flawed parts of our country's legacy that affect us all. There are repercussions and ripples from a large rock being thrown in a lake, ripples that affect us and our brothers and sisters, even if we weren't the ones to throw the big stone. We are all in the same lake, and thus affected. This understanding and admission will lead us to the first step of being aware and sensitive and will eventually allow healing to begin. God knows our motives and our hearts. If we act as though there was never a problem, we are saying that we are not interested in making anything better. We are also denying the truth that not only did slavery and racism exist in our country, but that the effects of slavery and racism are still being seen. Do not deny that; it is everywhere. It will take a full church effort to get there, but with Jesus as our commander, we can make the necessary progress. We have more in common with those in the household of faith in Jesus, because we have the Holy Spirit, than in any other bond this side of heaven. Those who are mature in Christ can help those who are immature seek reconciliation and a godly framework of understanding. The more our identity is based solely in Christ, the more we will be able to relate to others in a God-honoring way. White people will have the wisdom to counsel white people, and black people will have the wisdom to counsel black people. And we can become the brothers and sisters together that God wants us to be. White people, within the church, who have the flawed legacy, whether or not they are responsible for it, need wisdom. Should a person of German descent, who meets and befriends a Jew in the marketplace today, be void of empathy? Can he say, "*I was not a part of the Holocaust, so I do not need to feel empathy for what my people, my country, did to you.*"? Of course not. His attitude should include an admission of what was done in the past and sympathy towards those who were wronged. This would show the heartfelt disapproval of the actions that took place. Otherwise, his attitude is indifference, and indifference is not love. Our nation's collective past is a part of our legacy. We need to speak with each other. These conversations must start in our individual relationships as we realize that people are hurting today from things said today. They are also hurting today from a lack of sensitivity, or lack of admission of the past, by those who are called brother and sister. Ask God for opportunities, and then listen actively to someone who shares how they have been hurt. Do not form an opinion; just hurt with them. They are not making up the hurt. The feelings are real. When my wife is hurt, her feelings are genuine. Sometimes we just need to listen. This will give them an outlet while reassuring them that not everyone is quick to speak evil words. Negative words are like piercing arrows or sword thrusts. It is the tongue of the wise that brings healing, and for those who have been wounded, there can never be too much reassurance or love. Be a proactive friend by listening across the table.

People may be reading this from alternate perspectives and multiple bases of knowledge. Just as we all have different levels of biblical knowledge, we also have different historical and experiential knowledge. If you or a family member has been on the receiving end of discriminatory comments or actions, that is a historical and accurate situation, and your experience is valid. If you have in your family line a relative who gave his life and blood fighting for the freedom of black men and women, that historical situation is also accurate, and that experience valid. As we increase our knowledge of God and His Word, we will learn principles of relating to one another and can more easily disseminate historical knowledge so we can grow together. When we understand another's situation, our appreciation of them and their perspective grows, because we have gained knowledge about where they speak from. Let us listen and have a soft heart about the things that have happened in the history of our country that have hurt the black race. Families were separated and the effects are still seen in their descendants. There will come a time to discuss some of the courageous historical events in which white and black people have done selfless things for one another, side by side, some even giving up their very lives, with a heart of devotion and love to God and their brothers.

I have six wonderful children. I cannot focus on each of them completely at each moment. I do not want to, and thankfully I am not called to. As my children grow, they become more and more talented at certain things. If one of my children spends time learning to ride a bike, I may be impressed and compliment them in front of the whole family, and that is good and right. To say, "*Wow! I am so impressed with you, and you are so good at riding your bike; great job!*" may be an affirmation to them that grows their courage and makes their heart smile because they are being talked about. It is human nature for another child to respond competitively: "*I'm good at riding my bike too; I can ride faster than so and so! I learned to ride my bike 6 months younger, and I can beat them in a race.*" It is the "*Hey, make me the center of attention*" syndrome, or as Toby Keith would say, "*I wanna talk about me!*" Let's not be the children of God who divert attention back to ourselves when one of our siblings is put in the spotlight or is having their feelings validated. Listen. Be patient. We must go against our inclination to talk about me. Listen together, hurt together, and grow in knowledge together. This will make our relationships tighter in Christ. If we are empathizing, great. If we are invalidating someone else's hurts because we want to talk about how our hurt is greater, or about how we are being misunderstood, it shows we really do not care about that person's hurt. Inside the Family of Equal Standing, there will be plenty of opportunity to listen to one another and grow together. Let's take turns. There are as many perspectives as there are people.

Chapter 11

The Orphan

Psalm 68:5 tells us that "*God is the Father of the fatherless.*" The first time I really captured the essence of this verse, my heart was touched with the love of our Father in heaven. What a great God, full of vast love. He cares for those in great need. He cares for the orphan, and He leads them to godly homes. He does this by stirring you and me to give them a physical home while teaching them about the love of Jesus so that they may find rest in their eternal home, heaven, because they have faith. Trust in Jesus is the most important thing we pass on to the next generation. It is our job to teach them. As Christians, we believe that God's promises extend to a thousand generations of those who love Him and keep His commandments (Exodus 20:6). We may understand equal standing and how it applies to friendships, abortion, evangelism, and cultural differences in the church, but have we thought about how it applies to those most intimate relationships in our immediate family? When we think about having children, do we assume that all of our children will be biological ones, or do we consider adopting children from near or far who need a home? Adopted children are equally grafted into our families, and God's promises apply to all of our children, whether adopted or biological. Taking a step of faith and adopting needy or otherwise abandoned children provides powerful opportunities to live out and exemplify the concept of equal standing on a daily basis.

Romans 10:14-15 says, "*How then will they call on him in whom they have not believed? And how are they to believe in him of whom they have never heard? And how are they to hear without someone preaching? And how are they to preach unless they are sent? As it is written, 'How beautiful are the feet of those who preach the good news!'*" (ESV). Just as we speak truth to our biological children, we have an extraordinary opportunity to speak truth to adopted children.

Unless you have been an orphan, you cannot grasp what it is like to be one. I cannot understand from personal experience, but I can understand spiritually from Scripture, for I have gone from a life without God to a life with God. When I see God's rich love lavished upon me, I realize that He did not leave me alone. He did not leave me as a spiritual orphan to wander without guidance. Satan wants to keep our young ones wandering. He wants them to live without God so that they never become a part of Christ's kingdom or an influence for it. Thankfully, I have never felt unwanted. Perhaps because I experience the fierce grip of God's love on my life and the blessings of an earthly family's affection, it saddens my heart all the more for those who are spiritual and physical orphans. They do not have what we have.

When Sarah and I were in the process of adopting our daughters Sadie and Adeline from Ethiopia, my father reminded us that we were missionaries, and that adoption has a strong potential return on investment. Certainly, God does all the work in bringing children to a saving faith in Him but placing them in a family where they will hear, be taught, and understand the truth of God and His Word is a promising beginning. Raising children is one of the largest and most profitable missionary endeavors we undertake. Being a stay-at-home mom and teaching the truths of Jesus is one of the most influential jobs under heaven.

We have all seen the infomercials on TV that show the starving children of the world, with their ribs showing and their bellies bloated from a lack of nutrition. When I saw these as a child, they had a great impact on me, and I suspect that they did for you too. But let's focus on the spiritual realm for a moment. We do not know all the details about God, but we know what He has told us about Himself in His Word. God Almighty has said that He is a Father to the fatherless. Therefore, we know that He cares for all of His creation. We also know that he provides for our physical needs as His children. Psalm 37:25 says "*I have been young, and now am old, yet I have not seen the righteous forsaken or his children begging for bread*" (ESV). Often, God provides for the orphan through His people, by asking us to take on His mission. But the ultimate purpose of our existence is that He might provide for our spiritual needs through Jesus Christ. Jesus says in John 14:18, "*I will not leave you as orphans, I will come to you*" (ESV). Every human being desperately needs Christ. Whether royalty or orphan, black or white, male or female, we are all spiritual orphans without Jesus. We are blessed to recognize our need for Jesus, but many do not. Imagine the impact in just a few generations if we all adopted an orphan and God used that to save them. Within three or four generations that one child that you adopted could have a family tree of twenty to thirty bright lights for Jesus Christ. Imagine the results if the world-wide church of Jesus did this! Satan loves the idea of uncared-for children, left alone as orphans both physically and spiritually. As Jesus continues to build His church, the gates of hell will not prevail against it. It is time for us to possess the enemy's gates!

I believe that humanitarian efforts to feed these children should be of utmost importance, but if these children die apart from Christ and are lost forever, the enemy wins. Satan wants to destroy children by whatever means necessary. He wants to busy adults so they do not notice. He wants them aborted. The thief came to steal, kill, and destroy, and as the number one proponent of abortion of all time, he wants children viewed as a nuisance and an inconvenience. As a fellow believer, I ask you to consider opening your home to a child, or to speak up and encourage those around you to do so. God is the Father to the fatherless, and He uses real people like you and me to do His work here. It is not just about providing clean drinking water and food to children, although that is so important. It is about providing the gospel of Living Water and the Bread of Life that changes a child forever.

Of all the things God has allowed me to accomplish by His grace alone, raising children, biological and adopted, is by far the most fulfilling. I get to pray for them each day. I get to shape their worldviews through God's Word and service to Him. In Deuteronomy 32:9, God calls His people His inheritance. As humans, we are often given an inheritance, and we value it. God is also interested in His inheritance, but His inheritance is His children, Christians, you and me. Why should we do anything else but involve ourselves in growing God's inheritance, and therefore His kingdom? He does the work, but He uses us. He does not need us, but He blesses us. God will provide for me, for you, and for the children of the world.

He is the Father to the fatherless. He is the provider. We are not. He will always provide the means for anything He calls us to do. You will understand this if you know the love with which He loves you. It is there even if you do not feel it or see it or know it yet. He has been my Provider for years. God provided throughout our adoption story. Early in the process, we received an unexpected gift towards our adoption cost. He also blessed my business during that time. My wife will never forget receiving a $14,850 bill from the adoption agency. She did not even bother calling me because it was such a large bill, and she figured that it would allow installment payments. That same day, I received two closing checks totaling over $15,000. This was the largest amount of income I had ever received in one day. I remember calling Sarah after the checks had come in, unaware of the bill she had just received. I said, *"I just wanted to let you know that I am holding two checks right now, for about $15,000. I have never had a day of work like this before, and I wanted to tell you."* She said, *"Well, that is good news because we just received a bill today for $14,850, and it sounds like that will cover it."*

As I look back on this time, God provided money for us at just the right moment, and he continued to provide all that we needed for our physical daily bread as well. Not everyone has the same experience. Perhaps your journey will be more amazing. Either way, our God is able to supply all of our needs according to His glorious riches in Christ Jesus. I am convinced that God will show Himself faithful to any parents who move forward with adoption. It is an issue dear to God's heart. When you bring a child into your home, you are saying that the faith He has blessed you with is worth sharing with someone who might otherwise never hear the gospel. Is there any other pursuit more worthy than praying that God will grow His family through you? This is one way to go into all the world and make disciples.

As I write from this side of adoption, the benefits and blessings are mine. Sarah and I have had people say to us, *"Wow, that is so great of you to adopt."* I can tell you that my heart echoes the prayer of Daniel, *"Not because of our righteousness but because of your great mercy"* (Daniel 9:18). It is Christ who has done something great, but somehow, He allows us to share in the joy of His work. We can provide a home to the orphan and share Jesus with our child. We have the best place to call home for these children because we know it will point them to the eternal heavenly home.

I am an advocate for children to be placed in loving, godly, Christian homes. These children are guaranteed to be taught the truths of Jesus, for that is what loving, godly Christian homes do. Without Jesus, they will be starving no matter how full their stomachs are. Feed one. I promise you that He who foots the bill for your current family has room to include one more at your table. God has given you the ability to make an impact for His kingdom. God tells us in James that true religion is to look after the orphan and the widow, so we can be certain that it is His will. You would not tell your wife, "*Let me pray today and see if it is God's will for me to love you.*" In the same way, you should not look at the orphan and pray "*Lord, is it Your will that I adopt?*" If we are not specifically called to adopt, we need step out in faith and help those who are. I pray that we are entering into the "*Adoption Age of the Church.*" It will take faith, but not blind faith. God has made clear in His Word what He supports. If God supports the fatherless, we should too. We will have the full support of our Father. Become the next adoptive parent, and let the table grow.

Adam Rebandt

Chapter 12

Marriage and Spiritual Gifts

"So God created man in his own image, in the image of God He created him; male and female He created them" (Genesis 1:27).

How we exist together in a marriage relationship, being so different from one another, is a vast mystery (Proverbs 30:19). But it is a mystery from God. He makes it beautiful. Scripture tells us that He has created marriage. A man leaves Mom and Dad and becomes one flesh with his wife. To understand what it means to have a faith of equal standing in our marriage, we must first understand that God has created both the husband and the wife in His image. This is fundamental because it helps us understand that we both reflect His glory.

We will look at marriage and spiritual gifts together, because understanding that God is the Giver of all good gifts will help us understand our equal standing before God in the marriage relationship. It will also help us understand that our roles are equal and important, although the gifts given to us by God for our roles may be different. First Corinthians 12:4-12 says,

Now there are varieties of gifts, but the same Spirit, and there are varieties of service, but the same Lord; and there are varieties of activities, but it is the same God who empowers them all in everyone. To each is given the manifestation of the Spirit for the common good. For to one is given through the Spirit the utterance of wisdom, and to another the utterance of knowledge according to the same Spirit, to another faith by the same Spirit, to another gifts of healing by the one Spirit, to another the working of miracles, to another prophecy, to another the ability to distinguish between spirits, to another various kinds of tongues, to another the interpretation of tongues. All these are empowered by one and the same Spirit, who apportions to each one individually as He wills.

God gives what God gives to each individual. He gives wisdom to one and knowledge to another. In the marriage relationship, He gives the role of husband to one; He gives the role of wife to the other. They both have an equal part in the relationship so that marriage does not exist one without the other. In the same way, God has given the parts of the body in the church so that we do not exist without one another.

Comparing our gifts, both in the church and in the marriage relationship, can create unnecessary confusion. We may bend towards jealousy if we begin to look at things through our eyes rather than God's eyes. This can lead us astray. What God has given us in marriage and in spiritual gifting matters more than what God has given us compared to what He has given others. He has given us an equal standing, and we are equally responsible to do all we can with what He has given us.

When Sarah and I were in our first few years of marriage, we got together regularly with several other couples. We played board games, and one night one of the husbands stated, "*My wife is the only one here that does not have a job making x-dollars per year, so it makes sense that she would not know how to play this game.*" He was saying that she was not intelligent enough to play the game, that because she did not have a well-paying job she was not worth as much. He was not joking, which would have been bad enough. He was being demeaning. This is not a way to talk about a partner of equal standing, and it is also not accurate. Fifteen years later or so, I am not sure that this couple is still together.

The world will consider one partner more valuable if they contribute more financially. Since they bring in more money, their decisions have more weight. But this is not how God designed us. Money is only good for this life. It does not have much value when compared to the spiritual blessings of Christ Jesus. I have also heard it said that income is your post-school report card. I believe that God's report card has a grade scale more concerned with our spiritual growth. God has given us the ability to raise children, to discipline with love, to guide, to teach, to set an example, to maintain order, to lead devotions, to feel what others feel, to clean, to show hospitality, to be a great friend, to be an encourager, to be full of joy, to listen to our spouse, to speak gently, to weep with those who weep, to snuggle and cuddle with our children and have them know they are loved, and to put others first as we find our energy in Him. Every one of those gifts is equally important. God uses them for His glory in whatever time and place He chooses.

We share an equal role even when it comes to the children we have. There is not a marriage that produces biological children without both a man and a woman. I have heard children say something along the lines of "*Dad, if only you would have married someone taller, then I wouldn't be so short*," not realizing that the very existence of that child is predicated upon the exact combination of Mom and Dad. Likewise, your spiritual gifts would not be yours if God did not give them to you.

We might ask how we can be content with what God has given while at the same time desiring growth in other areas. God responds when we ask Him what matters to Him and what He wants to accomplish and are willing to be used by Him for His glory, for He wants us to desire His ways. Maybe you aspire to be in church leadership or involved in a church ministry, and you think that it would only be possible if God had gifted you differently. God has given some an incredible ability to sing and lead worship, but this does not mean that we must all have that ability in order to be equal, or that God will not move some along in their growth to be in that position one day. We must be content in our gifting, not envious, and we must ask God to show us what our gifts are and how to use them for His glory. We are guided by our faith in Jesus Christ, His Word, and prayer. Let us ask God to lead us, for that is when He brings us to situations that mold and shape us into the believers that He wants us to be.

We have become too good at comparing ourselves to others and at worrying and complaining. We are not good enough at being grateful in our relationship with Jesus. It is Jesus who guards our hearts against all lies from

Satan. God is real. Even when we know this to be true, we may live as if we do not believe it. We tend to live as if He has given us a faith of unequal standing. If we believe that we have a faith of equal standing, then we must have a faith of understanding. Husbands and wives must love each other. If you feel like you are superior to your spouse, know that you are not. Husbands and wives are joint heirs of eternal life. We will both have the same reward of eternal life, enjoying the river of life that flows from the throne of God.

There is a song by Francesca Battestelli called "He *Knows My Name*." A line in that song says, "*I don't need my name in lights, I'm famous in my Father's eyes*." Ironically, Francesca Battestelli is famous in the Christian-music world, and she has her name in lights on a regular basis. We might look at her and say, "*Well, of course she can say that. It is much harder to say that when your name is not in lights*." Yet when we stop to think about it, we know exactly what she means. She is saying that she does not care about earthly fame, and if God took it all away or never gave it in the first place, she would still have everything she ever needs in Christ. This is how it is for every believer in Christ, and we need to be reminded of it.

If you live in a 1,500 square-foot house, but your neighbor Joe lives in 2,500 square-foot house, you might be envious of him and wish that you had that house. But what if tomorrow God gives you a 2,500 square foot house? You will not want Joe's house because yours will be equally great. Our problem was never with Joe. Our problem was with God. We question why God has not given us the same blessings He has given others. Why has God not given me a marriage like so and so? Why has God not given me friends like so and so? Why has God not given me a life as easy as so and so?

This envy creeps into the church and the area of spiritual gifting as well. But we might not have the spiritual maturity to handle the blessings that others have. One of the greatest signs of a spiritually mature Christian is gratitude about others' spiritual gifts along with thankfulness for one's own spiritual gifting. This is possible when we know we already have the gift of a faith of equal standing. There is no other gift that compares, physical or spiritual. When you see a brother or sister in Christ receive something great, you can be truly happy for them and still content with what you have. You can truly rejoice in others' blessings. Pay close attention to how you react when someone around you is blessed, publicly praised, receives a nice gift, or buys that new vacation home on a lake. Often, our hearts are not in the right place. Our reactions are all visible to God, and they reveal the state of our hearts. Ecclesiastes 12:13-14 says, "*The end of the matter, all has been heard. Fear God and keep his commandments, for this is the whole duty of man. For God will bring every deed into judgment, with every secret thing, whether good or evil.*" God knows our thoughts. Humility comes before honor. Begin asking what God thinks about your thoughts and actions. See if they align with His will. He will lead, guide, and appoint. Use your gifts to bring Him glory, even in secret, and even through menial tasks. "*Whatever you do, work heartily, as for the Lord and not for men, knowing that from the Lord you will receive the inheritance as your reward. You are serving the Lord Christ*" (Colossians 3:23).

This faith of equal standing will give husbands and wives and every member of His church, each with different gifts, an equal inheritance. We will all see Jesus face-to-face. If that is what we are living for, then we will be filled with joy and full of thankfulness. If we are ungrateful and jealous, what does that say about our focus? Maybe we have become too fond of this world and entered into a love relationship with things. If we love the things of this world, how can the love of the Father be in us? Our love and our heart must be stayed on God, the One we claim to serve.

Let us love our spouses, seeking their best, not insisting on our own way, empathizing with them, rejoicing with them, and sharing in their successes. A marriage is godly when the wife's and the husband's hearts align with God's. For this to happen, we must view our spouses as equal. Husbands and wives are given from God. Rejoice in your present circumstances, for they are good! You get sixty or so heartbeats per minute, 3600 per hour. Maybe a couple of things went wrong today, but many more have gone right. God's blessings are forever if you are His child. All things, at every moment, work together for good.

Focus on Christ. Plead with Him if you desire anything in your life to change. Read His Word, and you will desire to please Him and to be more like Him. Your thoughts will be consumed by Him, by His glory and radiance.

There will be less and less time to think about yourself. His radiance will change you. "*Those who look to him are radiant*" (Psalm 34:5a). If we are not radiant, then we are not looking to Him. He gives His radiance freely, and it is equally available to all, no matter our role in the home or church. We can each look up and see Him, and when we do, everything else fades away.

Chapter 13

God's Equality Act
vs.
Satan's Equality Act

We look up to God by giving Him authority. "*And the king took off his signet ring, which he had taken from Haman, and gave it to Mordecai…*" (Esther 8:2a, ESV). The signet ring represented the king's authority. As a seal, it held the place of power for those who held it and used it. You could look at the king's signet ring as "*Thus says the king.*" In Genesis 41:42, Joseph, with the pharoah's signet ring, was given the authority of the king: "Then *Pharoah took his signet ring from his hand and put it on Joseph's hand… Thus he set him over all the land of Egypt*" (ESV). So, who really has authority, and where do we find it? I recently had a week away with the basketball team that I coach. We studied God's Word together and lived together, all while enjoying some high-level basketball competition. We studied the repeated phrase in Genesis 1: "*And God said,*" a phrase questioned by Satan only two chapters later when he asked, "*Did God really say?*" (Genesis 3:1, ESV) Is there a holy signet ring?

In a day and age with such a high degree of offense, frustration, and gender and racial issues, we need to discover where the blame lies, then see if we are a part of the daily problem or part of the solution. When God created man in Genesis 1:27, God's Word, the Divine Signet Ring, said, "*So God created man in his own image, in the image of God he created him; male and female he created them*" (ESV). Wow. God made you and me in His image, distinct from beasts, which were not created in His image and thus do not have a soul. But He did give one distinction: He created them male and female. This authoritative distinction is a gift. Sadly, we have come to disregard the Creator's Signet Ring; that is, what He has said, when we attempt to blend genders together or cross over from one to the other. We only discover our true worth when we understand how the Creator made us. God's Word doesn't say, "*He made only women,*" or "*He made only men,*" or "*black and white He created them.*" We make those distinctions; God never did. Neither blackness nor whiteness nor any other trait is dominant but being made in God's image is incomparable. We have His mark, His image, on us. As the Old Testament period neared its end, God said in Haggai 2:23 "*On that day, declares the Lord of hosts, I will take you, O Zerubbabel my servant, the son of Shealtiel, declares the Lord, and make you like a signet ring, for I have chosen you, declares the Lord of hosts.*" Since Jesus has died, risen, and sent His Holy Spirit, we as believers are now marked with His seal to bring His authority, His Word, to people.

The problem of incorrect and blurred distinctions started with fallen angels and man's sin. Before anything, God was here. No angels, no Satan, no man, no fallen man. Just God. Then He created the angels for worshiping Him. They have a glorifying role, praising God for who He is and acting as His messengers, helping and aiding mankind, whom He subsequently created. Isaiah 14:13-14 reveals Satan's attitude: "*I will ascend to heaven; above the stars of God I will set my throne on high; I will sit on the mount of assembly in the far reaches of the north; I will ascend above the heights of the clouds; I will make myself like the Most High*" (ESV). He aims to be equal with God. Satan lured Eve and continues to lure mankind into this temptation: "*For God knows that when you eat of it your eyes will be opened, and you will be like God...*" (Genesis 3:5, ESV). The promise of awakening is alluring: "*you will have a new level of understanding. The moment you go against what God already told you, you will have new vision, and be like God. You too, can have equality with God.*" But the cost of thinking that way is death.

The devil works the same way today, and his goal is to steal, kill, and destroy. He is not trying to steal candy from the store, kill a spider, or destroy a building. He wants to steal your soul, kill your body, and destroy your hope of eternal life with God. How does he do this? Very few people line up for it knowingly. He does it through deception. We may even call it the deception and confusion of equality.

When God speaks, His Word, His Signet Ring, has absolute authority. When God created male and female, He spoke. Satan comes along and attempts to confuse truth using God's vocabulary. He suggests that a woman should be allowed to be a man, and a man should be allowed to be a woman. But God already put His signet ring and authority on that man, creating him a man, and on that woman, creating her a woman. But in our society, we are told that you aren't kind or treating people with equality if you refuse to let them be who they want to be.

Satan does not care about equality. Satan tempted towards and supported the 3/5ths mentality, abortion, hatred, and separation. He desires to have equality with God in order to rewrite what God has said. He wants equality in order to make the rules and equality in order to rewrite the rules. He wants equality between creature and Creator. But God has spoken. Psalm 14:1 says, "*The fool says in his heart, 'There is no God'*" (ESV). In his attempt to be God and strive for equality with God, Satan is in effect saying that there is no God. God is Supreme, and when we discard what He has said, we are saying there is no God, and we become like Satan, likened to a fool by God's Word.

As one sealed with the Holy Spirit, my spiritual eyes are opened. So are yours, if you know Him. We no longer fear man, who can kill the body, and after that can do no more. We already know the deepest longing of the soul of the ones who oppose us. We know their deepest need because it is the same as ours. The difference is that ours has been filled. This gives us a love to point to the real enemy: Satan, the enemy of us all.

You and I will die, and so will everyone we know. Look around you; it is happening everywhere. Satan has been watching and deceiving generations of people since Adam and Eve. When our peers die, he moves on to new ones. If he can persuade us to end life in the womb, he will do it. If he can make us hate each other, man versus man, leading to death, he will do it. If he can tempt a generation of men and women to fill up with pleasures and can trick them into thinking they don't need Jesus when they die, he will do it. All along, he knows full well that you, being tricked, will one day see how he stole your soul and destroyed you.

Gender is a key to identity because God made it a distinction between people. He created you the way He did, and your uniqueness is a gift. My identity is found in Him who made me, not in how I feel. There is so much gender mis-identity in our world right now, and we wonder how people do not know who they are as they try to find themselves. The God who spoke to create the world made you who you are. His hand formed and fashioned you. Satan comes along and says, "*God did not fashion and form you. Believe that He did not form you, then your eyes will be opened, and you will be like God, deciding good and evil.*"

Jesus Christ is the bridegroom, and we are the bride. God does not give us permission to switch genders and become our own salvation. Our identity is in what He has done. When we float into thinking that we do not need Him, we move into an identity crisis because we weren't created to work that way. He is the only One who saves.

When someone starts picking apart the Bible and suggesting that there is an error or issue with something in God's Word, there is usually a deeper question underlying the criticism of the seeming contradiction: "*Has God really ever spoken anything, ever, that is relevant to man?*" This question is just another form of the enemy's starting line of temptation: "*Did God really say?*" We are called to think things through. Look around you, and look at creation. Isaiah 55:7 says, "*Let the wicked forsake his way, and the unrighteous man his thoughts*" (ESV). God calls us to disassociate ourselves from our bad thoughts. We can love a person even while explaining that they need to disassociate from their bad thoughts. This is not harsh. People and their views are so intertwined today that they have in many ways become one with their views. I am a person, and my mind has the ability to think and change. I am not one with my thoughts. Scripture teaches that unrighteous people should forsake their thinking, put it at arms' distance, turn, and run the other way, never coming back.

God always gets the last word. There are so many examples in Scripture of God turning evil for good, and even changing the perspective of those in authority. It can happen, and it does happen, because of who God is. When Babylon conquered Judah, they took many Jews captive and brought them to Babylon. There were proud leaders, such as Nebuchadnezzar, whom God humbled, who then proclaimed God in his personal life. But there was also the law of the land and the kingdom of Babylonia and Persia. When God decreed hundreds of years before the Babylonian captivity that a king named Cyrus would come and send the Jews back to rebuild Jerusalem, it happened. After the work began, those who opposed the work of rebuilding contacted King Artaxerxes. The king then ordered the building to stop, in opposition to the Word of God that had been spoken. This slowed the Jews down, but they eventually continued rebuilding according to God's decree, not man's. Darius became king after Artaxerxes and did the work of digging up the history of Cyrus's decree that the Jews be allowed to go back to rebuild Jerusalem and the temple there. When Darius saw the letter from Cyrus, he allowed the work to continue. The heart of a king is like a waterway; the Lord directs it wherever He wishes. Darius, whether or not he realized it, was giving credence to what God had already said. But this last part is what I love about God. After His people had faced large opposition to the rebuilding from those who ruled over them, he sent Darius, who not only allowed them to rebuild, but had a holy fear of the Lord in him. Listen to what he says in Ezra 6: 10-12:

> *"That they may offer pleasing sacrifices to the God of heaven and pray for the life of the king and his sons. Also I make a decree that if anyone alters this edict, a beam shall be pulled out of his house, and he shall be impaled on it, and his house shall be made a dunghill. May the God who has caused his name to dwell there overthrow any king or people who shall put out a hand to alter this, or to destroy this house of God that is in Jerusalem. I, Darius, make a decree; let it be done with all diligence" (ESV).*

It makes me wonder if, in Darius's search for the records of Cyrus, he read about how God humbled Nebuchadnezzar and Belshazzar and showed His power! In any case, God can use the pride and pomp of those opposed to him to create the opposite effect in those who become humble when they see how

He deals with the proud. My prayer is that those who desire equality with God to "have a say" other than what God has said, will see Satan's heart of deception, his pride, and subsequent humbling, and that they will quickly run the other way and humbly turn so that they do not end up like him. Why must you be stubborn and die to find out that you are not equal with God?

For those in authority, particularly in governments and school systems, God is someone to be feared. There will be an "uh-oh" moment for each of those who rush headlong towards ungodliness that promotes leading children astray. Matthew 18:6 says, "*Whoever causes one of these little ones who believe in me to sin, it would be better for him to have a great millstone fastened around his neck and to be drowned in the depth of the sea*" (ESV). I cannot imagine promoting and misleading children into false beliefs and encouraging gender mis-identity. It is like raising a hand in God's classroom and saying with brazen face, "*I desire destruction and discipline as I go against what You have said, God.*" The same goes for the abortion movement, and any teaching that goes against what God's Word says. It is equality with God that they seek, but in the end, it is equality with Satan that they get. I want the "they" to be a small number. I want people to turn. I want godly churches. I want godly school boards. I desire fewer people ending up with Satan at the time of their death. Keep sharing the Gospel. Keep sharing the Good News. No one is too far gone to be left out of hearing the message. They might just be like King Darius or Saul. You do not know to whom God will reveal His truth. He does it through His Word, delivered through you, a bearer of His Signet Ring.

Chapter 14

God's Family of Equal Standing – A Call to Action

What do you weep for? What do you really, really, weep for? Do you weep for your bedtime snack of vanilla ice cream topped with chocolate ice cream? Maybe you are weeping over the fresh loss of one dearly loved: a husband, a wife, parent, sibling, grandparent, or friend… maybe even a child. None of us can stay the hand of the Almighty or challenge His counsel as to the "why." We must find satisfaction in the "Who." God orchestrates all things to the praise of His Glory. Maybe you weep over your lot in life, being overburdened with the weight of providing for your family, and it is just hard. Perhaps it is your health or the health of a loved one, and you cannot do anything to change it, or take the pain away. Sometimes our weeping might be selfish; we feel sorry for ourselves for not getting that boat, car, house, job, husband, wife, child, promotion, easy life, or for not having that _____(fill in the blank, whatever else) that was given to someone else. My friends: don't. As we look through Scripture, reading it cover to cover, we will see the Heavenly Father whose love for His children extended to giving us equal standing in His sight because of Jesus. Satan and the powers of darkness would have us redefine and mar God's love, purposefully seeking to ensnare us by causing us to measure God's love materially, rather than spiritually and eternally. It is so easy to do, but my dear friends, do not fall to that trap. I have seen, from tasting, that God's love is real, and that He is all that we need. Although we know this is true, we are weak humans, and all who have ever lived have at one time or another wept for themselves.

Hezekiah, king of Judah, is a scriptural example of a godly man weeping selfishly. We find his story in II Chronicles. In chapter 29:3 we are told, "*In the first year of his reign, in the first month, he opened the doors of the house of the Lord and repaired them.*" Hezekiah immediately restored that which was taken away by his father Ahaz, who had shut up the doors of the temple of God and who had made alters in every corner of Jerusalem, making offerings to other gods. Hezekiah then called all of the priests and Levites (the priestly tribe of Israel) and gave them three responsibilities. They were to consecrate themselves, consecrate the house of the Lord (the God of their fathers), and carry out the filth from the Holy Place. He then commanded them to not be negligent, explaining, "*The Lord has chosen you to stand in His presence, to minister to Him, and to be His ministers and make offerings to him.*" (II Chronicles 29:11) Incredibly, all of this was done by the 16th day of Hezekiah's reign as king. In the first year of his reign, the first month of his reign, and by day 16, this was accomplished. As soon as this work was completed, "*Hezekiah the king rose early and gathered the officials of the city and went up to the house of the Lord*" (II Chronicles 29:20, ESV). Hezekiah turns to the Lord early in his reign and early in the morning. He will also turn to the Lord early in trial and adversity.

Sennacherib, the king of Assyria, opposed Hezekiah and opposed the Lord: "*do not listen to Hezekiah when he misleads you by saying, 'The Lord will deliver us.' Has any of the gods of the nations ever delivered his land out of the hand of the king of Assyria?*" (II Kings 18:32, ESV). When Hezekiah heard this, he tore his clothes and headed directly to the house of the Lord. He didn't grab a Newcastle lager from the fridge, watch his favorite TV series on his ipad, indulge in his favorite dessert, or grab a smoke; he went right to the house of the Lord. Isaiah the prophet then brought Hezekiah a Word from the Lord: "*Do not be afraid because of the words that you have heard, with which the servants of the king of Assyria have reviled me. Behold, I will put a spirit in him, so that he shall hear a rumor and return to his own land, and I will make him fall by the sword in his own land*" (II Kings 19:6-7, ESV). Sennacherib taunted the Lord again, sending a letter to Hezekiah telling him to not trust in the Lord for deliverance. Sennacherib then listed the many kings whom he had destroyed and implied that because their gods could not deliver them from his hand, the Lord would not be able to deliver Hezekiah from Sennacherib's hand. Again, in adversity and trial, Hezekiah went to the house of the Lord. He spread out the letter he received in God's presence. He acknowledged that God is the true God, and that He reigns. He also acknowledged before the Lord that it was true that Sennacherib had laid waste the kings of the earth. But Hezekiah saw a flaw in the Assyrian king's claims. Sennacherib said that God was not able to deliver Hezekiah. Hezekiah took this lie, brought it before the Lord, and pleaded with God to deliver them for the sake of His Name, so that by this deliverance the nations of the earth might know that gods of wood and stone cannot deliver, but that the One who made heaven and earth can. The Lord, the Dread Warrior, is with us. Our persecutors, therefore, will stumble and will not overcome us. Hezekiah was familiar with God's Word, and God responded to him through Isaiah the prophet regarding Sennacherib: "*I know your sitting down and your going out and coming in, and your raging against me. Because you have raged against me and your complacency has come into my ears, I will put my hook in your nose and my bit in your mouth, and I will turn you back on the way by which you came*" (II Kings 19:27-28, ESV). God continues, "*By the way that he came, by the same he shall return, and he shall not come into this city, declares the LORD. For I will defend this city to save it, for my own sake and for the sake of my servant David*" (II Kings 19:33-34, ESV). That night, God did an awesome work as He sent His angel and struck 185,000 dead in the Assyrian camp. Sennacherib returned the way he came, and went back to his hometown. "*And as he was worshipping in the house of Nisroch his god, Adrammelech and Sharezer, his sons, struck him down with the sword*" (II Kings 19:37, ESV). Where is the god of Sennacherib? Do not believe that the god of Sennacherib will save you, for he was no god at all.

The account of Hezekiah is important because it helps us to think through issues of justice and righteousness in terms of what is important to God versus what is important to us. Hezekiah faced many challenges, and Scripture is clear that Hezekiah sought the Lord early in his reign, early in the day, and early in trouble. But now, Hezekiah would face his greatest battle to date: his own mortality. II Kings 20 gives us the details. Hezekiah became so sick that he was at death's door. The Lord said to Hezekiah, "*Set your house in order, for you shall die, you shall not recover*" (II Kings 20:1, ESV). Hezekiah immediately prayed to the Lord, weeping bitterly. He wept bitterly and cried out to God: "*Now, O LORD, please remember how I have walked before you in faithfulness and with a whole heart, and have done what is good in your sight*" (II Kings 20:3, ESV). God was under no requirement to answer this prayer, but He did. I have read this story many times since I was a child, but verses 4 and 5 jumped out at me on my last read through the Bible. "*And before Isaiah had gone out of the middle court, the word of the Lord came to him: 'Turn back, and say to Hezekiah the leader of my people, Thus says the LORD, the God of David your father: I have heard your prayer, I have seen your tears. Behold, I will heal you. On the third day you shall go up to the house of the LORD*'" (II Kings 20:4-5). God immediately answered Hezekiah's prayer: immediately. I had always pictured this story as though Hezekiah spent prolonged time in mourning and anguish of soul until God was finally gracious to him, heard his cry, and answered him. For God to say to him, "*You are going to die,*" and then while the prophet Isaiah was still walking back from delivering the notice of impending death, to hear Hezekiah's prayer, to see Hezekiah's tears, and to promise and affect healing, is simply astonishing. But this is our God! He answered Hezekiah's prayer right away and without hesitation. Three days later, Hezekiah again found himself in the presence of the Lord, in the temple, where he had been many times before.

There are at least two things to take note of in this section. One is that God answered such a big prayer immediately. Wow! The second is the selfish nature of Hezekiah's prayer. Hezekiah was concerned about himself alone. During this time he showed all the treasures and storehouses of his kingdom to the king of Babylon, presumably boasting of his wealth. Do you remember who conquered Judah? It was Babylon. Isaiah then prophesied to Hezekiah that all that was in his (Hezekiah's) house and all that which his fathers had stored up till that day would be carried off to Babylon. This would have been bad enough, but it gets worse. "*Nothing shall be left, and some of your own sons, who shall be born to you, shall be taken away, and they shall be eunuchs in the palace of the king of Babylon*" (II Kings 20:17b-18). This is the one thing in Hezekiah's reign that has always bothered me, and it should bother you too. Hezekiah's response to Isaiah confirms his self-centeredness: "*The word of the LORD that you have spoken is good.*" *For he thought, "Why not, if there will be peace and security in my days?*" (II Kings 20:19).

The consequences of our selfishness often have the greatest impact on those who come after us. Hezekiah cared only for himself. He did not consider those who came after him. He thought, "*Hey, at least my life will have peace and I will be able to enjoy my abundant extended life.*" But it was God who worked a miracle and gave him this extra time on this earth. Better thoughts would have been, "*Perhaps I should live my life for what matters to God... God, what are the desires of your heart? Will you give Your desires to me? I would like my desires to line up with your desires, Lord! That is why I am here on this earth anyway.*"

All I can think about at this point is justice and righteousness: the things of God's heart compared to our own selfishness and focus on the "*me.*" Our thoughts should turn from ourselves to our treatment of one another, to those who cannot speak up for themselves, to children, and to our spouse, all of whom are made in God's image. God's children, and all of those made equally in His image, matter greatly to God. Deuteronomy 32:9 reminds us that "*the LORD's portion is his people, Jacob his allotted heritage*" (ESV). Add up, for example, the grandeur of the Grand Canyon, the trees in Sequoia National Forest, and the beauty of Maine and the East Coast. They all bring glory to God! But just one child means more to God than all of the other parts of His creation because he or she is made in His image and has an eternal being. Places will not last; they will be gone and destroyed one day. But each generation of people has eternal souls. God cares about His children, for they are made in His image. If this is important to God, more than the beauty of the other things we see around us, how is it not important to us as well? Can you think of anything that should be a greater priority to us than the love, nurture, upbringing, and caring of those walking the path with us and who will come after us? Our distracted lives combined with those who oppose God make this battle difficult. With prayer, this must change and change quickly on our watch. It is time for us to call upon our Dread Warrior of Jeremiah 20:11 to lead us to victory in justice and righteousness. Victory comes from Him, and this is His fight. If I see those around me in church leadership or influential spheres of life trampling upon His Word, I will pray they become tremblers at His Word or that their responsibilities be replaced with those who do tremble. And we need more tremblers, droves of us who refuse to give up, sit on the couch, or go to our grave without doing all we can to see our churches and land look more like God's revealed desires. Do we want the Dread Warrior to fight this battle? Then we must tremble and take His Word seriously. We saw how Hezekiah's pride after being healed had tremendous consequences of not caring for those who came after him. Spiritually, we have also been healed. We are called to more than seeking our own good in our life. We need to seek the good of those around us, our brothers and sisters of equal standing, and those who will come after all of us. Jesus, our King of Kings, is the best example of this.

Before our Lord raised Lazarus from the dead, we read that "Jesus wept" (John 11:35, ESV). This was a shedding of tears kind of weeping. Why was Jesus still weeping when he knew He would soon raise Lazarus from the dead? Of course, Jesus had human emotions, and seeing his friends moved could have moved him. There may be more to it, however. Two verses earlier, Jesus was "deeply moved" in His spirit. This word, "*ebrimaoma,*", includes the idea of indignation. The same word is used in Mark 14 when a woman poured pure nard on Jesus' feet and those around her unfairly and harshly rebuked her. Jesus had a deep groaning against His enemy Death, for He was soon going to defeat it, not only by raising Lazarus, but in going to the cross. When Jesus wept, indignantly grieving over the evil of death, He took action right away and rose Lazarus from the dead. When Jesus cares about something or someone, He has the power to act immediately on their behalf. The night Jesus was betrayed in the garden, we are told that "*being in an agony he prayed more earnestly; and his sweat became like great drops of blood falling down to the ground*" (Luke 22:44, ESV). Jesus was in so much agony that an angel from heaven appeared to Him, strengthening Him. We are called to be "*looking to Jesus, the founder and pefecter of our faith, who for the joy that was set before him endured the cross, despising the shame, and is seated at the right hand of the throne of God*" (Hebrews 12:2, ESV). When Jesus was in agony and asking the Father if it were possible that this cup pass from Him, His drops of blood were sweating for those He had called, that we might have a way back to the Father.

The indignant Jesus humbled Himself. Unlike Hezekiah, He was thinking of all of God's children, including you and me, who would come after Him. The ultimate act of pride is caring about oneself at the expense of others. It is arrogance to avoid facing the consequences of our current actions on future generations. When we refuse to confront racism or a lack of justice in the church and promote our equal standing in Christ, we are saying "*I don't care about you.*" When someone has an abortion, they are saying, "*I care about myself and my life. I do not care about that which comes after me.*" This person has no understanding that it was God's choice alone to grant conception in the womb. Abortion is the absence of wisdom about Who made the choice. God hates child sacrifice, and the scriptural penalties for it are severe. As a nation we have sacrificed and mistreated our black and Native American brothers and sisters, and we continue to sacrifice those whom we as a nation consider less valuable, including the unborn. Yet all along God has said we are equal. Jesus weeps over America. He weeps when He sees our land. We quote "With *Liberty and Justice for all,*" but our nation has failed to live up to this motto. What on earth can we do about it? When I look at people, I am not confident of a solution. But the Holy Spirit who lives in us enables us! Jesus works through us, cares, and is able. We may wonder why He is not doing anything in America right now to completely heal race relations or why He hasn't overturned Roe V. Wade. But the problem is not Him; it is us. His will is going to be accomplished, and He is just. If we want Him to hear our prayers, then we must fervently listen to what He has to say. Our attitude must be that of Samuel, who even as a child said, "*speak Lord, for your servant hears*" (I Samuel 3:9, ESV).

In the last chapter of Isaiah, God talks about everything He has made by His power. He manifests His Almighty power, but then He says, "*this is the one to whom I will look: he who is humble and contrite in spirit and trembles at my word*" (Isaiah 66:2, ESV). In America I see a sentiment among those in the church and in the land of fearing what will happen if we speak out against something that God hates. For God to answer us and move us in unity, we must tremble at His Word. Our problem is that we do not tremble at His Word, but instead we trample the very Word of God underfoot. To be silent during our short time on this earth is to allow His Word to be trampled upon. We have a cannibalistic society, which allows parents with an unwanted baby to cut off the next generation. They care about their own life, and not that which comes after them. The human race, black and white cultures together, needs to get into the Word, putting aside the false ideologies and false gods that we have made in our minds. We must be unified in the knowledge that God made us equal, and we must help build the next generation. One way we do this is by disallowing racism and abortion to be accepted in any form, for they contradict our faith of equal standing, which includes the entire human race, whether black and white or brothers and sisters in the womb. Lord willing, we will be able to see some of the fruits before God calls us home. Stop trampling and start trembling at the Word of God, and He will bring us through this time with great victory as we recognize that being made in the image of God heals black and white relationships and extends to our protection of the unborn. I am convinced of this because of who He is. It is in His character; He will aid us. Psalm 56:8, ESV says, "*You have kept count of my tossings; put my tears in your bottle. Are they not in your book?*" God has a bottle storing all your tears, your tossings, and your agonies. Is it filled with tears for yourself and the things you do not have? There are legitimate times to ask God to fulfill our needs and of course we can ask him for anything, but friend, how often do we fill the tear bottle with the same things that God weeps for? We have such a limited time here to accomplish what He calls us to, and if we are always thinking about ourselves, will we really gain anything our whole lives? But if in unity we ask the King to accomplish what matters to Him, I believe He will answer because our desires have become His desires. It is possible.

When God separated the nations by language because of their sinful ways at the Tower of Babel, he said, "*Behold, they are one people, and they have all one language, and this is only the beginning of what they will do. And nothing that they propose to do will now be impossible for them*" (Genesis 11:6, ESV).

The New Testament provides us with a contrast to this disruption of unity, for Jesus has come to unite everything to Himself, both things on heaven and things on earth. If we as the church become one with the one Holy Spirit on what matters to the One, nothing will be impossible for us. We will be unified in thought, mind, and purpose, led by our Dread Warrior into battle fighting for the things that matter to Him. If we as a church refuse to let the enemy's division and death guide our nation, I believe God will do something about it, through us, His hands and feet. He will help little hands and feet survive the womb and be added to a generation of those who love Him and keep His commands. If we become less interested in filling our wallets and bank accounts for ourselves, less interested in chasing and craving comforts for ourselves, and more interested in filling our tear bottles for Him and for others that He has called us to care for and love, then anything can be accomplished. He is able to do abundantly more than all we can think or ask. Let us focus on praying the desires of Jesus back to Him. We will have a unified church, caring for our brothers and sisters of equal standing simply because we know that it is God's heart. We will care for life and advocate for life even if the sole reason is because we know it matters to God. When God says that He made us in His image, He made us equally in His image. Black or white, man or woman, in the womb or out of the womb, God has made a wonderful choice for life. It was His choice, His image, His forethought, His knitting together in the womb. Each human being is a person, fearfully and wonderfully made, whom God knows by name. His Word and Name attest to this. I am amazed as I look around and see our society embodying injustice, standing for abortion, and standing contrary to God in so many ways. The will of man will always stand opposed to the will of God. Therefore we who have the Spirit of God living in us must show the rest of society the way. It must start with us as a church. There is only One to whom we can look, for the norms of society and even our laws accept child sacrifice, which God hates. We are to trust Him whose Name is Faithful and True, and partner with Him as He undoes the spiny claws that the enemy has wrapped around the ideologies of our country. Jesus is at work, and He told us that He will do great things through us. Is this one of them? It certainly lines up with His desires and revealed Word. I am grateful for the many godly leaders in our nation, but they cannot do it alone. We have kept change from coming by not being consistently and daily opposed to the evil in our land.

We must be daily warriors, battling hard in increasing our knowledge of God's Word and our voice for righteousness, and in fervent prayer to end evil ideologies that impact real lives, many of which have ended in the time it takes to read this book. We desire to see the human race, including black and white people raising one voice for the lives that God has already chosen to give to children in the womb, become a nation and world of Christians who view one another in the faith as those with an equal standing. This opposes what the flesh and natural man seek. We need God's Spirit to lead us.

We must have tenacity for God's desires on earth. When the prophet Elisha had a final conversation with King Joash, Elisha said,

> *"Take a bow and arrows." So he took a bow and arrows. Then he said to the king of Israel, "Draw the bow," and he drew it. And Elisha laid his hands on the king's hands. And he said, "Open the window eastward," and he opened it. Then Elisha said, "Shoot," and he shot. And he said, "The Lord's arrow of victory, the arrow of victory over Syria! For you shall fight the Syrians in Aphek until you have made an end of them." And he said, "Take the arrows," and he took them. And he said to the king of Israel, "Strike the ground with them." And he struck three times and stopped. Then the man of God was angry with him and said, "You should have struck five or six times; then you would have struck down Syria until you had made an end of it, but now you will strike down Syria only three times." (II Kings 13:15-19, ESV).*

There was not something magical about striking the ground 5 or 6 times as opposed to 3. The point is that the king stopped. How many times have we as Christians prayed for something only to stop asking God for help, victory, or answered prayer? We must keep asking Him for His victory. When we take the attitude of "*Well, I've prayed for this and it hasn't come to pass, so what's the point?*" or "*If God really cared about changing the world in this way He would have already done it,"* we put ourselves in God's sovereign chair and allow seemingly unanswered prayer to dictate what we ask God for or stop asking him for. We do not believe that we serve the same God who immediately healed Hezekiah. When we see strained relations between black and white people, or we see child trafficking still existing in our country, or we see abortion on the rampage, we have to remember that we have hope because God Himself stands against these things. God is in charge, controls all things, and will accomplish the things that bring Him glory and are according to His will. He will give us courage and grace to carry out His plan.

I am ready, willing, and able to fight for this every day until I see the face of Jesus. Will you join me? My brother or sister of equal standing, remember this: that Dread Warrior from Jeremiah 20:11, the One Who holds the sword, the One feared and dreaded, is on our side. He stands opposed to everything contrary to His Name and Word. I do not want to oppose what He says. Can you imagine standing before the Dread Warrior and saying to Him, "*Because he is black, I am better than this one. Because they are still in the womb, they are dispensable people or not people at all. Because I care so much about myself and my comforts, I did nothing about it.*" No. Let's fight on our knees together with our hands held high to God, asking Him to bow his heavens and come down! Come to our aid, God! David cried this way many times. Perhaps, even in this life, we will be able to say in the same way as David after God gave him rest from all his enemies: "He bowed the heavens and came down" (Psalm 18:9, ESV). God did it; He answered. He has said that we are created in His image, and that because of faith in Jesus, we are equal. All life matters, including yours, for it is the Spirit of God that gives it.

Things are moving towards the end. We are closer to the return of the Lord than we have ever been. When God blessed Abraham in Genesis 22, He told him that his offspring would possess the gate of their enemies. Abraham's son Isaac was born, and God found Isaac a wife named Rebekah. As Rebekah's family was sending her off to marry Isaac, "*they blessed Rebekah and said to her, 'Our sister, may you become thousands of ten thousands, and may your offspring possess the gate of those who hate him!*'" (Genesis 24:60, ESV). When Jesus came to earth hundreds of years later, He said, "*And I tell you, you are*

Peter, and on this rock I will build my church, and the gates of hell shall not prevail against it." (Matthew 16:18). And a few decades later Paul wrote, "and if you are Christ's, then you are Abraham's offspring, heirs according to promise" (Galatians 3:29, ESV).

Dearest brothers and sisters, we are that church that Jesus is building against which the gates of hell will not prevail. The promise that we are Abraham's offspring has been fulfilled. We are the church, and we will possess the gate of His enemies. Let's go to the gate; our Dread Warrior is already victorious there and has given us a sword (the very Scriptures that can tear down strongholds) to wield. It was Peter who wrote to those who have obtained a faith of equal standing, and it was to Peter that Jesus said He would build His church, and that the gates of hell will not prevail against it. It's time to possess the enemy's gates as Jesus' church. And the enemy is Satan. Let's go!

Adam Rebandt was married to his wife, Sarah in 2002. They have six children of equal standing, a mix of boys and girls, biological and adopted, black and white. He enjoys walks with his wife, waking early to spend time in the Word, coaching basketball, and sharing meals with family and friends.

Adam Rebandt and Family

R. Adam Rebandt III is available for interviews and personal appearances. For more information contact us at info@advbooks.com

To purchase additional copies of these books, visit our bookstore at:
www.advbookstore.com

*A*dvantage
BOOKS

Longwood, Florida, USA
"we bring dreams to life"™
www.advbookstore.com

www.ingramcontent.com/pod-product-compliance
Lightning Source LLC
Chambersburg PA
CBHW062006040426
42447CB00010B/1945